NUMBER THREE

EASTERN OREGON

PORTRAIT OF THE LAND AND ITS PEOPLE

By Alan D. St. John

AMERICAN GEOGRAPHIC PUBLISHING
ALL RIGHTS RESERVED
WILLIAM A. CORDINGLEY, CHAIRMAN
RICK GRAETZ, PUBLISHER
MARK THOMPSON, DIRECTOR OF PUBLICATIONS
BARBARA FIFER, PRODUCTION MANAGER

This series provides in-depth information about Oregon's geographical, historical, cultural and natural history subjects.

Library of Congress Cataloging-in-Publication Data

St. John, Alan D.
  Eastern Oregon : portrait of the land and its people / by Alan D. St. John.
      p.   cm. -- (Oregon geographic series ; no. 3)
    ISBN 0-938314-49-1 (pbk.) : $14.95
    1. Oregon--Description and travel-- 1981- -- Guide-books. 2. Natural history--
Oregon--Guide-books.   3. Oregon--Description and travel--1981-   I. Title.
II. Series.
F874.3.S69 1988
917.95'0443--dc19   88-26222
                                                                          CIP

ISBN 0-938314-49-1
Text © 1988 Alan D. St. John

© 1988 American Geographic Publishing, Box 5630, Helena, MT 59604
(406) 443-2842
Design by Len Visual Design; Linda Collins, graphic artist.
Printed in Hong Kong by DNP America, San Francisco.

To my family:

My mother and father, who passed on to me a love and respect for the land; and my wife and son, who patiently understood when field work and research often usurped our time together.

ACKNOWLEDGMENTS

In writing the text of this book I had help from a number of people whom I would like to thank.

The librarians at Deschutes County Library and Central Oregon Community College Library and Mary Fiorillo of Eastern Oregon State College Library, who all helped me more than they can know by locating reference materials.

A special thanks goes to Dr. Ewart M. Baldwin, of the University of Oregon, who read the entire geology section and gave me a number of excellent suggestions for improvements. Several other issues were further clarified by geologists Larry Chitwood and Bruce Nolf. Botanist Dave Danley read the flora section and engaged me in a fascinating and lively discussion, clarifying the ecological differences between high deserts, low deserts and steppes. Scott Stuemke, District Archaeologist for Deschutes National Forest, answered many questions concerning aboriginal prehistory. Faye Waheneka, of the Warm Springs Confederated Tribes Information Center, gave me a number of valuable insights into Native American culture.

Several people helped me with historical data and locating historical photos: Bob Boyd, Illea Jones, Forest Cooper, Caryn Throop, John Scharff, Betty Renk, Grace Bartlett, Duane Alderman, Don Franks, John Philip Brogan, Jim Anderson, and Susan Seyl of the Oregon Historical Society.

Caxton Printers, Ltd. kindly gave me permission to use the Reub Long quote from *The Oregon Desert*.

And, as the saying goes, last but certainly not least, my wife, Jan, read through the entire text as I wrote it and offered honest, constructive criticism and positive support.

Alan D. St. John is a writer/naturalist living in Bend. He has researched and roamed the landscape of Eastern Oregon for 20 years, spending the last 10 as a contract field researcher for the state's department of fish and game. He has written about the special qualities of the Oregon high desert and the little-known mountain ranges of eastern Oregon for major Oregon publications and national wildlife publications.

PREFACE

Where does a writer begin in attempting to describe a region like Eastern Oregon? How do you convey the sights, sounds and smells? The feel of it under your feet? The rich assemblage of flora and fauna? The personalities of the people and their communities?

It's easy to overuse adjectives when trying to impart a sense of the awe and freedom that sections of this land can stir in a person's heart—gazing off the rim of Steens Mountain's Kiger Gorge; rafting the rapids of the Deschutes River; sitting by a sagebrush campfire under a starry High Desert firmament; cresting Glacier Pass on a Wallawa back-packing trip; watching transfixed as hundreds of ducks suddenly take to startled flight at Malheur National Wildlife Refuge; hot-air ballooning in silent flight alongside an eagle as it soars above the snowy summits of the Three Sisters Mountains. Words often can seem frustratingly inadequate and only hint at the real thing.

Nevertheless, perhaps it was all summed up best by a first-time visitor to the area. While doing consulting work in 1984 for Fuji Broadcasting during the filming of the Japanese television series, *From Oregon with Love*, I happened to ride out to the location with one of the directors. I speak no Japanese and he spoke very little English. After ascertaining through a short, monosyllabic conversation and sign language that he had toured parts of Eastern Oregon, I asked him what he thought of it all.

There was a moment of silence while he intently searched his mind for a way to express his impressions. Then, he decisively spread his arms wide and said with strong conviction, "big!"

CONTENTS

Front cover: Strawberry Mountain, viewed across the John Day River Valley near Prairie City. LARRY ULRICH
Back cover: Springtime fields near Milton-Freewater. DAVID JENSEN
Title page photo: Sunrise paints the Jordan Valley. BRYAN PETERSON
Facing page, left: Crook Glacier, viewed from the southeast, nestles within Broken Top in the Three Sisters Wilderness of the Cascade Range. JEFF GNASS
This page, left: Lush Buena Vista ponds in Malheur National Wildlife Refuge disprove the stereotype of Eastern Oregon as a monotonous expanse of desert. LARRY ULRICH

3

INTRODUCTION

Above: *This calf on the Jordan Valley's Fillmore Ranch knows how wet Eastern Oregon can be.*
TIM THOMPSON
Right top: *The Arlington Grain Elevator on the Columbia River testifies to the agricultural wealth of Eastern Oregon.* BRYAN PETERSON

Everyone chuckles at Oregon jokes, the ones dripping with the infamous rain of the Pacific Northwest.

"Last year 267 Oregonians fell off of their bicycles and drowned."

However, non-Oregonians who believe these good-natured jibes have certainly never toured the entire state. With broadened familiarity comes surpirse; then a sense of wonder at the amazing variety of terrain within this one state's boundaries. In reality, the mono-climate of dank mosses and misty, green rain forests that supposedly carpets the entire state exists only in the geography of the imagination.

The Cascade Mountains divide Oregon into two dramatically different climates and terrains, but somehow that fact does not travel as well outside of Oregon as jokes do. To the west of this north-south mountain range, legendary precipitation does nurture a mild, lushly vegetated environment. To the east of these moisture-trapping mountains, though, lies a high and dry land of sunny, open pine forests, rugged canyons, expansive sagebrush plains and arid deserts.

What especially surprises newcomers is the extent of this dry, high country. One third of the state lives up to its rainy reputation. The remaining two thirds comprise a huge, excitingly diverse region collectively known as Eastern Oregon.

This area is hardly a parched, monotonous sagebrush expanse, broken only occasionally by buttes sprinkled with a few tenacious, wind-bent junipers and pines. The variety of topography is astounding. Three geographic sections unfold east of the Cascades: Central Oregon, Southeastern Oregon and Northeastern Oregon. Each has its own distinctive geology, flora, fauna, people and flavor. Woven together, those three sections make Eastern Oregon an immense tapestry of contrasts, colored and decorated with sagebrush, juniper, pine, aspen, lava, snow-capped granite peaks, lakes, rivers, desert sand dunes, coyotes, antelope, deer, rattlesnakes, eagles, squirrels and much more.

Within this intricate tapestry certain colors predominate in each regional section, creating the sights, sounds, smells, textures and movement of life that denote each respective region: lava flows, rushing rivers and juniper forests of Central Oregon; sagebrush-covered plains, basin deserts and fault-block ranges of Southeastern Oregon; the towering, pine-clad, white granite crags and glacial lakes of Northeastern Oregon.

Unlike the gentle, green contours and mild climate of Western Oregon, this is a harsh, dramatic and invigorating land. It does not invite mellow repose and contemplation as do the soft, grassy western woods and glades. This strong, decisive environment stimulates activity. The weather may fluctuate from warm and sunny, to cold, snowy and windy all in one day. Immediacy is the watchword here!

Comparatively sparsely settled, the land itself is the most dominant influence. Consequently, the people of Eastern Oregon are hardy, robust, outdoor-oriented folk with attitudes and values strongly shaped by their surroundings. And, like the multifaceted region in which they reside, Eastern Oregonians include many types, ranging from Native American Indians to cattle ranchers, farmers, loggers, businessmen, artists and teachers, to the retired elderly, who come to the area for its dry, sunny, healthful climate. Fishing, hunting, skiing, river-running and other outdoor sports inspire passionate devotion.

Eastern Oregon's exciting scenery and bracing climate compel residents and visitors alike to venture outdoors and explore. Each turn in the trail or road brings changing vistas and the unexpected.

Indeed, with an intensely blue Eastern Oregon sky overhead, the heady aroma of sagebrush in the air, and the beckoning calls of magpies in the junipers, who could resist becoming better acquainted with Oregon's dry side?

COLUMBIA GORGE
NATIONAL SCENIC AREA

THE
DALLES

COLUMBIA R.

PENDLETON

WENAHA R.

HELLS CANYON
NATIONAL RECREATION
IMNAHA R.

MT. HOOD

BARLOW
PASS

LA GRANDE

ENTERPRISE

MATTERHORN
PK.

EAGLE CAP
PK.

GRAND RONDE R.

WALLOWA
MTNS.

NORTHEASTERN
REGION

DESCHUTES R.

CENTRAL REGION

BLUE MTNS.

BAKER

ELKHORN MTNS.

MT. JEFFERSON

MCKENZIE
PASS

OCHOCO
MTNS.

PRINEVILLE

JOHN DAY R.

JOHN DAY

GREENHORN
MTNS.

SNAKE R.

THREE
SISTERS

BEND

MAURY MTNS.

ALDRICH
MTNS.

STRAWBERRY
MTNS.

CASCADE MTNS.

BACHELOR
BUTTE

PAULINA MTNS.

NEWBERRY
CRATER

ONTARIO

SILVIES R.

MT.
THIELSEN

BURNS

MALHEUR LK.

MALHEUR R.

FOSSIL LAKE

SOUTHEASTERN
REGION

CRATER LAKE
NATIONAL PARK

WINTER RIDGE

YAMSAY
MTNS.

ABERT LK.

HARNEY LK.

JACKASS
MTNS.

SHEEPSHEAD
MTNS.

OWYHEE R.

SUMMER LK.

STEENS MTN.

MT.
MCLOUGHLIN

UPPER
KLAMATH
LAKE

ALVORD
DESERT

CATLOW RIM

GEARHART MTN.

WARNER
LKS.

HART

BEATYS
BUTTE

KLAMATH FALLS

LAKEVIEW

GOOSE LK.

PUEBLO
MTNS.

TROUT CREEK
MTNS.

PART I

Land of Dynamic Diversity

Above: Subtle colors and dramatic shapes infuse Eastern Oregon's overwhelming expanses. Here a mule deer buck pauses at the horizon.
BRYAN PETERSON
Right: Eastern Oregon joins extremes of topography, from basin deserts to fault-block ranges, from Mann Lake (in the distance) to the moonscape of East Rim Viewpoint (foreground) on Steens Mountain. LARRY ULRICH

To the first-time explorer of Eastern Oregon, this broad, expansive land can be an overwhelming, even intimidating, experience.

To senses accustomed to lushly wooded, gentle countryside or urban surroundings, the rugged, often harsh landscapes and climate of this region take some getting used to. But in a short time, with greater familiarity, the intriguing qualities and untamed beauty of its deep chasms, wild rivers, seemingly endless deserts, and lofty, alpine mountains begin to work their beguiling magic. The temptation to see and know more of this land proves irresistible. And the natural heritage of this section of the Pacific Northwest is a rich one to explore. Although large portions appear barren and lifeless at first, closer examination reveals a remarkable variety of flora and fauna adapted to these dry, high elevation ecosystems.

Successfully blocking a large portion of the wet, moderating air moving inland from the Pacific Ocean, the Cascade Mountains create a pronounced rainshadow effect to the east. While some locations in the humid coastal forests of Western Oregon can record 128″ of rain in a year, the arid Alvord Desert in Southeastern Oregon may receive as little as 7″. Milder temperatures generally prevail to the west of the crest, while the intermountain region of Eastern Oregon claims a more typical continental climate with hot, dry summers and cold, snowy winters. Consequently, much of this area, popularly referred to as the "High Desert," supports scant vegetation.

According to the technical definition of a desert (evaporation seven to 50 times greater than precipitation), most of the open country of Eastern Oregon actually falls under the botanical classification of semi-arid to arid "sagebrush steppe." The rather nebulous, catch-all High Desert definition lumps together an enormous drylands area of the West containing grasslands and sagebrush steppe, sparse juniper woodlands, the basin deserts, marshlands and fault block mountains. Thus, although not strictly botanically correct, this vivid name provides a handy local and historical package for an otherwise unwieldy variety of ecosystems.

Whatever the proper terminology, when compared with Western Oregon's damp, heavily wooded landscape, much of the eastern part of the state appears decidedly desert-like. Two completely different worlds co-exist within the state of Oregon, one of misty, balmy breezes, born of the wide sea and delicate, verdant growing things...the other of high, dry desert winds, bearing the tang of juniper and sage and the echoes of spacious solitude.

Above: Snow tinted by a February sunset skirts sagebrush and junipers on BLM land near Drinkwater Pass, Harney County. JEFF GNASS
Left: A springtime view of Mt. Hood from south of The Dalles. D.C. LOWE

Geologic Underpinnings, Shifting Climates & Fossil Records

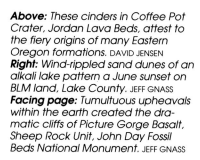

Above: These cinders in Coffee Pot Crater, Jordan Lava Beds, attest to the fiery origins of many Eastern Oregon formations. DAVID JENSEN
Right: Wind-rippled sand dunes of an alkali lake pattern a June sunset on BLM land, Lake County. JEFF GNASS
Facing page: Tumultuous upheavals within the earth created the dramatic cliffs of Picture Gorge Basalt, Sheep Rock Unit, John Day Fossil Beds National Monument. JEFF GNASS

In order better to understand why Eastern Oregon differs so dramatically from the western parts of the state, we must look far back into the prehistoric past and trace the history of the foundations of the entire region

It will help if we can radically alter our perspective for a few moments. Imagine that you are hovering several miles above Oregon with a grand view of it all. Also imagine that you have regressed in time to a period about 200 million years ago. One of the first things glaringly apparent from this ancient vantage point is that most of what we now call Oregon does not exist, except as the floor of a shallow sea. The present western edge of the North American continent has not yet moved into its present position.

Although most theories regarding the origins of present-day landforms constantly differ and change, the theory of plate tectonics has achieved wide and stable acceptance. In a nutshell, the concept holds that our seemingly rock-solid continents are not as firmly fixed as they appear. Like an egg with a badly cracked shell, the crust of the earth is divided into a number of gigantic pieces, called plates. Geologists subdivide these into two basic types: one, the oceanic plates, submerged underwater and built of densely hardened lava that wells up from cracks on the ocean floor; the other, thicker continental plates composed of less dense varieties of rock. Both oceanic and continental plates slowly (an inch or two a year) float about the planet atop dense interior rocks so super-heated by the earth's molten interior that they are like soft, malleable clay. This floating is called *continental drift*. When huge sections of the earth's crust collide and grind against each other, colossal events unfold.

When the North American continent broke away from what is now Europe and Africa and moved westward, somewhat more than 200 million years ago, a geologic phenomenon—*subduction*—began to create Oregon as we know it today.

Quite simply put, the North American continental plate is moving over the top of the heavier Pacific oceanic plate. The floor of the Pacific Ocean is slowly being engulfed by our continent and absorbed into the bowels of the earth.

When the Pacific plate began its slide under the continent, sedimentary debris scraped off the disappearing ocean floor accumulated along the seam. This accumulation slowly built a coastal range of mountains. Concurrently, a parallel volcanic chain of mountains formed some distance inland.

The earth's crust is only about 60 miles thick. As the Pacific plate angles downward, it eventually reaches the hotter depths of the earth under the continent, at a point about 100 miles inland. Oceanic plate materials then melt, rise along vertical fractures in the earth's crust, and eventually erupt as volcanoes.

Theoretically, as the continental plate has gradually drifted westward, this process repeated itself whenever the subduction zone relocated. Slowly, new coastal extensions formed Oregon's modern coastline, Coast Range Mountains and the interior volcanic Cascade Mountains.

However, as with most seemingly clear-cut theories, there are often more complex influences that also contribute to the whole picture. Geological investigations into the transformations that have produced Eastern Oregon are extremely difficult, as most of the evidence from the distant past has been completely covered and hidden by more recent lava flows. A scientist must put together a geological puzzle while many of the puzzle's pieces are lost under the table he works on.

Above: *An August sunset highlights eons of layer-by-layer sedimentary deposits in Painted Hills Unit, John Day Fossil Beds National Monument.*
JEFF GNASS
Right: *Dry desert air now preserves the casts and molds of marine fossils.*
KARNA STEELQUIST

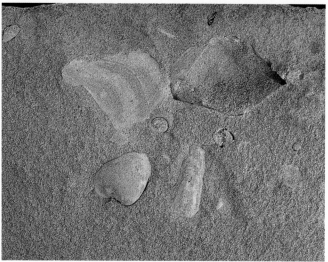

What *is* known is that around 200 million years ago the coastline of Oregon was located far to the east, probably in the vicinity of what is now the Oregon-Idaho border, possibly swinging southwestward into Southeastern Oregon.

A relatively recent theory adds a new piece to the puzzle. This concept maintains that *displaced terranes,* ancient groups of tropical islands in the middle of the Pacific Ocean, radiated outward, slowly moved along by continental drift on smaller subsections of the continental plates (miniplates). These exotic islands eventually "docked" onto the prehistoric coastlines of various continents and were incorporated into these larger landmasses. For example, the Wallowa Mountains of Northeastern Oregon contain tropical fossil corals, mollusks, algae and sponges that are identical to those found in the European Alps. Paleomagnetic evidence and other clues also suggest that certain land masses in Europe, Southeast Asia and the North American Pacific coast may all share a common origin. If correct, this theory indicates that the westward-building process of subduction had help from these roving islands and bits of continents in building the West Coast. Oregon, therefore, may be composed of a conglomeration of original sea beds, rock from distant locations and lava flows.

One incredibly active volcanic period helped structure Eastern Oregon (and also covered most evidence of earlier formative periods) took place about 14 to 28 million years ago. Nothing in Oregon's long geological history matches its magnitude. During this fiery period, volcanoes and huge cracks belched forth a series of megafloods of lava that literally covered nearly all of Oregon east of the Cascades. Initially, a combination of lava eruptions and blanketing ash laid down the Clarno and John Day formations in the Blue Mountain area. Following this, about 14 to 16 million years ago, an even larger flow of basalt lava covered most of the remainder of Eastern Oregon. Some experts postulate that 80 percent of this lava poured out in a 2-million-year period. When it ceased, only the highest peaks of the Blue and Wallowa mountains protruded above an enormous plain of basalt.

Following this period, the Cascade chain began a phase of vulcanism that created the high Cascade crest. By this time, Oregon had assumed the same general form that we see today. However, other forces worked during the past 10 million years to refine and shape this huge basalt plain into the modern-day variety of geologic landforms that exist east of the Cascades.

In Southeastern Oregon, large north-south fractures in the basalt lava plain caused huge sections to uplift and tilt. Classic examples of these *fault block mountains* include Steens Mountain, Warner Mountain and Abert Rim. In some situations, where two faults ran closely parallel, the land between dropped, forming a *graben*, a basin valley bordered on each side by rock escarpments. The Alvord Basin below Steens Mountain and the Warner Valley below Hart Mountain typify this type of landform.

Changing climatic forces also sculpted the Eastern Oregon landscape. Most notably, within the last 2 to 3 million years, huge glacial ice sheets covered much of North America. South of these ice sheets, in Oregon, large, isolated glaciers formed at higher elevations of the Cascade, Blue and Wallowa ranges in the latter part of this ice age. Even Steens Mountain in Southeastern Oregon had its own glaciers.

Such glacial activity scoured out U-shaped canyons, often creating lakes behind the bulldozed earth that glaciers deposited—the *terminal moraine*—when the ice receded. Wallowa Lake in Northeastern Oregon provides a textbook-perfect example of this type of glacially-dammed reservoir, while Kiger Gorge on Steens Mountain exemplifies a very typical glacial canyon.

Extremely heavy precipitation also occurred during Oregon's glacial period. Run-off greatly accelerated the erosion of river valleys and canyons. The state's major river systems—such as the Columbia, Snake, Owyhee, John Day and Deschutes drainages—sliced their way through the lava plains, creating the large valleys, canyons and gorges we see today.

In the land-locked basins of Southeastern Oregon, large lakes formed, especially at the end of the ice age when the glaciers began to melt and recede. Today in the desert we see only the remnants of these huge bodies of wa-

Above: *The fault scarp of Abert Rim now helps impound Abert Lake.* DAVID JENSEN
Left: *Looking toward Mt. Washington from McKenzie Pass in the Central Cascade Range, where desolate lava lands stretch for miles.* JEFF GNASS

Above: *A dramatic formation of volcanic tuff at Leslie Gulch.*
GEORGE WUERTHNER
Facing page: *The Alvord Basin recedes into the breathtaking distance from East Rim Viewpoint, Steens Mountain.*
LARRY ULRICH

from the earth and carried away. Rocks known as *glacial erratics*, rafted by ice from distant Montana, remain visible today as far west as the Willamette Valley.

Over vast spans of time, such geological and climatic changes in Oregon gave rise to totally different ecosystems, each with its own flora and fauna. Then cataclysmic transformations like shifting continents, lava inundations, freezing ice ages and glacial floods, exterminated entire plant and animal communities while successive new lifeforms adapted.

The dominant animals inhabiting the area observed from our imaginary 200-million-years-ago viewpoint were Mesozoic-era dinosaurs. The climate at that time was mild and semi-tropical to tropical. A warm, shallow sea covered most of the region. Tree ferns and Ginkgo trees abounded. Then, by the beginning of the Cenozoic era some 60 to 65 million years ago, the dinosaurs had mysteriously disappeared, replaced by new and successful animals, the mammals.

The age of ancient mammals is recorded for us in the rock-layered pages of Oregon's various formations—most notably in the John Day country, one of North America's most important fossil-bearing areas. There, in the Clarno, John Day, Mascall and Rattlesnake formations, fossils evidence long periods of lush, subtropical climates supporting palm, fig, magnolia, redwood and cinnamon trees. Roaming these landscapes at various times were such exotic creatures as the primitive, four-toed, miniature horse *Eohippus*. Camels, tapirs, huge saber-toothed cats and giant rhinoceroses inhabited this land, and crocodiles swam its prehistoric swamps.

About 12 million years ago the Cascade Range grew high enough to begin altering the Eastern Oregon's climate. As its rainshadow lengthened, large areas of grasslands appeared. Animals adapted themselves to grazing: an ancestral form of the pronghorn antelope, and larger, more advanced types of horses, camels and deer. Massive mastodon elephants also moved through this ancient land of mixed open savannah and woodlands. With the coming of the ice age, around 3 million years past, towering woolly mammoths, woolly rhinoceroses and other cold-adapted creatures replaced those of the former milder periods.

By the close of the ice age, Eastern Oregon's climate and ecosystems had begun shifting to their present forms and spawning the flora and fauna we see today.

ter: Malheur, Harney, Abert, Summer, Warner, Goose and Klamath lakes. In extremely arid sections, only parched alkali flats, sand dunes and ancient wave-cut terraces bear stark testimony to these prehistoric lakes.

Throughout the ice age, giant dams of glacial ice formed in rivers to the north of Oregon, impounding gigantic reservoirs. Eventually, repeatedly, these blockages broke free and floods of mind-boggling proportions swept through what is now Northern Idaho and Eastern Washington, down the Columbia drainage, and into Oregon.

These deluges carried immense icebergs containing rocks and other glacial debris that acted like titanic battering rams, devastating everything in their paths. Whole forests, along with the soils they grew in, were stripped

Flora of Oregon's Dry Side

Above: *Sunset silhouettes a juniper tree near Bend.* D.C. LOWE
Right: *Wildflower blossoms enrich Barton Heights above Hells Canyon, where the Snake River traces the Oregon-Idaho border.* DAVID JENSEN
Facing page: *Pungent rabbitbrush and golden aspens decorate Fish Creek Valley near Steens Mountain.* LARRY ULRICH

The diversity of plant forms east of the Cascades makes understanding Oregon's natural history somewhat difficult. Further complicating the picture, a multitude of interlacing valleys, basins and mountainous country produces a confusing network of open, lower-elevation ecosystems surrounded by higher, forested ecosystems. Nevertheless, some basic distinctions prove helpful.

Over the years, various scientists have attempted to organize Oregon's many natural components of geology, climate and flora/fauna relationships into various bioregions. These multifaceted systems of physiographic regions and life-zones can be complex and are beyond the scope of this book. For our purposes, Eastern Oregon consists of three basic regions. Despite some mingling of ecosystems, each geographical region demonstrates a distinctive natural history.

No less than large geological landforms, plants give each region its own look, aroma and "personality." The map on page 16 depicts the major vegetation zones of Eastern Oregon, including the general distribution of plant communities.

Probably the most distinctive geographical region, Southeastern Oregon contains broad stretches of open rangelands broken by dramatic upthrusts of fault block mountains and rimrock-edged plateaus. This seemingly desolate country at first appears to nourish only one plant: sagebrush. But closer examination reveals many other types of vegetation adapted to this dry, open landscape.

The other common shrub of Oregon's dry-lands, rabbitbrush, can be differentiated from sagebrush by its distinctly different odor. While sage gives off the pleasantly aromatic, herb-like aroma that most people associate with the desert, rabbitbrush has a very unpleasant, pungent smell, reflected by its scientific name, *Chrysothamnus nauseosus*. Despite its disagreeable odor, however, rabbitbrush adds great beauty to the open country of Eastern Oregon when it blooms with a mass of small, bright sulphur-yellow flowers in late summer and early autumn, creating a sweeping, golden-yellow blanket of vegetation in the warm glow of a setting sun.

Alongside these shrubs grows a variety of native grasses such as bluebunch wheatgrass (bunchgrass), Sandberg's bluegrass, Idaho fescue and giant wild rye. Prior to cattle ranching, bunchgrass was much more abundant, but long-term heavy grazing and rangefire control helped sagebrush replace these grasses over extensive areas. However, some limited natural grasslands still survive in Southeastern Oregon.

Exotic grasses also have been introduced into the Southeastern Oregon ecosystems. The Bureau of Land Management, in an attempt to improve grazing conditions for cattle, uses herbicides in some areas to exterminate sagebrush, reseeding with Asian crested wheatgrass. Although these plantings provide more forage for cows, they preclude suitable habitat for many native animals that require more complex natural plant communities. For instance, the open, sandy areas between native shrubs required by desert lizards for running and foraging are being carpeted with introduced European cheatgrass, which also acts as tinder-dry fuel for summer

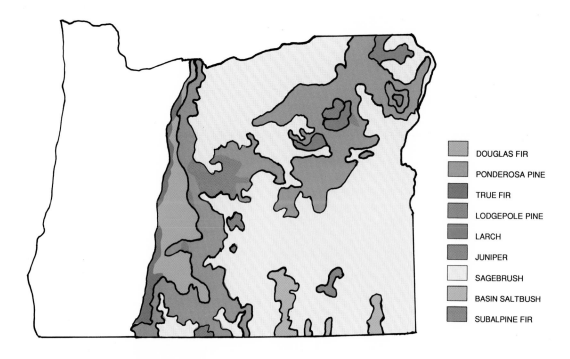

DOUGLAS FIR

PONDEROSA PINE

TRUE FIR

LODGEPOLE PINE

LARCH

JUNIPER

SAGEBRUSH

BASIN SALTBUSH

SUBALPINE FIR

Above: Prickly pear blooms enliven Hells Canyon National Recreation Area. DAVID JENSEN
Top: Major vegetation zones of Eastern Oregon. LINDA COLLINS

rangefires that sweep through thousands of acres each year. Similarly, the famous "tumbleweed" of American cowboy lore is also an introduced foreigner, the Russian thistle. Obviously, attempts at "improving upon nature" always trade off positive and negative results.

In the lower, arid basins and along the Owyhee and Snake river drainages, grow desert shrub communities typical of the Great Basin Desert. Though somewhat limited in extent compared to the sagebrush rangelands, these old lake beds and the sedimentary "badlands" canyon country, with alkaline, sandy soils, comprise the true deserts of Eastern Oregon. On baked dry slopes and at the edges of barren alkali flats and shifting sand dunes grow resilient desert shrubs like saltbush, shadscale, greasewood and spiny hopsage.

The Alvord Basin is the most arid example of a Great Basin Desert ecosystem in Oregon. It lies within double rainshadows, located not only far to the east of the Cascade Mountains but also leeward of the moisture-sapping bulk of 9,733' Steens Mountain. Several interesting desert plants, such as iodine bush and Mormon tea, find

the northern limits of their distribution in North America here.

Although usually associated with the deserts and plains, cacti are uncommon on these colder, northern drylands. Only two varieties, prickly pear and hedgehog cactus, occur at scattered localities in Eastern Oregon.

One obvious characteristic of deserts and grasslands is their lack of trees. A few varieties do grow in Southeastern Oregon, but only in limited quantities. The tree most successfully adapted to a dry climate, the western juniper, occupies higher elevations, often in association with mountain mahogany. A few small, isolated stands of ponderosa pine and Sierran white fir sprinkle high canyons on Steens Mountain. But conifers are a rarity in this arid region, as most species require 18" to 30" of yearly precipitation. Still, there are always exceptions: an unusual stand of ponderosa pine that grows in the open sagebrush country of northern Lake County where the rainfall averages only about 10". Forty miles from the nearest forest, these isolated trees have been dubbed the "Lost Forest."

At the margins of streams and springs, a limited variety of deciduous trees snaking along the watercourses stands out sharply against the drab, gray-green sagebrush surroundings. Willow, cottonwood and alder help green these riparian zones, but it is the beautiful quaking aspens, with their white bark and shimmering leaves, that capture the eye.

One of the special beauties of Southeastern Oregon is the sudden proliferation of delicate, brightly colored springtime flowers amidst the comparatively muted tones of this rugged land. If there has been ample precipitation throughout a winter, the sagebrush country can magically burst alive at this season with the blooms of arrow-leaf balsamroot, lupines, evening primrose, desert paintbrush, orange globe mallow, sagebrush buttercups, desert buckwheat, purple sage, scarlet gilia, dwarf monkey flower and a myriad of other varieties.

Although it may seem odd to include marshes in a discussion of open rangelands and deserts, in reality many wetland ecosystems share Southeastern Oregon's lake basins. The most extensive example, Malheur Lake, is actually a huge, shallow marsh. Lush growths of cattail, bulrush, burreed and Baltic rush provide nesting cover for thousands of migratory waterfowl. Similar habitats. exist at Warner, Goose and Summer lakes.

Clockwise from top left:
Paintbrush. JIM ROMO
Buckwheat. DAVID JENSEN
Lupine. STEVE TERRILL
No tree is better adapted to Eastern Oregon's dry climate than western juniper like this on on Steens Mountain. STEPHEN TRIMBLE
Mormon tea. STEPHEN TRIMBLE

17

Although the lower, open valleys of Eastern Oregon's other two regions share many of the same plant communities as the sagebrush rangelands and juniper woods, notable differences occur at higher elevations. Vast forests cloak the mountainous sections of the Central and Northeastern portions of Oregon.

Northeastern Oregon's forests of ponderosa pine, lodgepole pine, Douglas fir, grand fir, western larch and aspen exhibit many characteristics of the ecosystems of the northern Rocky Mountains. The plant communities of the Blue and Wallowa mountains also include many species found nowhere else in Oregon: limber pine, Rocky Mountain juniper, paper birch and Wallowa paintbrush. Other more widespread plants grow beneath these trees: pinegrass, bunchgrass, huckleberry, blueberry, bitterbrush, Rocky Mountain maple, squawbush and wildrose.

The Northeastern region contains some of the most extensive alpine areas in the state, particularly in the Wallowa Mountains. Stands of Engelmann spruce, subalpine fir and whitebark pine cling tenaciously to the high elevations of these white granite ranges. During the spring and summer months a colorful array of mountain wildflowers sparkle about the meadows and slopes like delicate, living jewels: golden and scarlet columbine, Rocky Mountain iris, pinedrops, sticky geranium, fireweed, shooting star, mountain bluebell and various penstemons.

Extensive, open grassland steppe zones punctuate the northern areas of this region, spread along steep canyon sides and benches of the Lower Grande Ronde, Imnaha and Snake rivers. The Columbia Plateau was originally covered with this same combination of bunchgrass and other native grasses, before its conversion to farming wheat and other crops.

Central Oregon, lying between the eastern slope of the Cascade Mountains and the western borders of the Blue Mountains and Great Basin, boasts a fascinatingly rich mixture of nearly all the ecological components found in Eastern Oregon as well as species more typical of the western valleys and mountains.

One of the most extensive forests of ponderosa pine in the world stretches north and south along the lower flanks of the Cascades. Lodgepole pine and small groves of quaking aspens are also intermixed, but the big, stately ponderosas obviously dominate. Bitterbrush, manzanita, snowbrush and pink spirea create a thick understory. At slightly higher elevations, Douglas fir,

white fir, grand fir and Western larch thrive. Along the shady, cooler canyons, such typically Western Oregon trees as red cedar, broadleaf maple and vine maple also grow.

Eastward from the mountains, the surroundings change rapidly as the dense, green forests end abruptly. Dry juniper woodlands, open rangelands, and broken canyon country covered by various grasses, sagebrush, and rabbitbrush mark the margins of the intermountain arid lands.

Although oak woodlands are found mainly west of the Cascades, these sturdy trees also range into parts of North- and South-Central Oregon. The Oregon white oak penetrates through the Columbia River Gorge into The Dalles area and then southward along the east slope of the Cascades to the vicinity of Maupin. Likewise, the white oak also spreads through the southern end of the Oregon Cascades, via the low canyons created by the Klamath River drainage. Other plant species associated with Western Oregon's oak woodlands also extend their distributions east of the divide in these areas—including the disliked poison oak, which often grows as a climbing vine upon these trees.

The northern sections of Central Oregon support extensive zones of the Columbia Plateau grasslands country. However, as in Northeastern Oregon, these former bunchgrass areas have given way to farming.

Farther south, the influence of Great Basin ecosystems affects Fort Rock, Christmas Valley, Silver Lake and the Klamath Basin, where various desert shrubs stubbornly survive in arid, sandy basins at the western fringes of this vast interior desert.

Above: *Fog shrouds oaks on Bald Butte.* D.C. LOWE
Top: *Evening sunlight graces the trunks of ponderosa pines on Black Butte in Central Oregon.*
ALAN D. ST. JOHN
Left: *Hot rock penstemon.* RON SPOMER
Facing page: *Thousands of waterfowl nest in marshes like this tule-thick slough on the Blitzen River, Malheur National Wildlife Refuge.* JEFF GNASS

19

Fauna of the Sagebrush & Pines

Above: *Western meadowlark.*
DAN DAVIDSON
Right. *Deer in velvet.* C.L. HANDY

The amazingly diverse ecosystems that spread across Eastern Oregon's mountains, canyons, deserts and grasslands support an equally diverse variety of animal species. Motorists speeding across the High Desert between Bend and Burns may not notice that an astonishing array of creatures, exquisitely adapted to this harsh environment, thrives in the sagebrush just off of the edge of the highway. Nevertheless, even from a fast-moving car, an interested observer will be rewarded with signs of life.

The large-eared black-tailed jackrabbit usually appears at night, attempting to cross roads. The white-tailed jackrabbit, less widespread, has become rare as its bunchgrass habitat continues to disappear. Pygmy rabbits and mountain cottontails show themselves less boldly.

Attracted by road kills, turkey vultures patrol in lazy, circular flights. Raucous flocks of large, shiny-black common ravens and beautifully iridescent black-billed magpies feed on carrion. Birds of prey, such as red-tailed hawks, kestrels (sparrow hawks) and golden eagles, perch atop utility poles and fence posts.

Oregon's sagebrush wildlife goes far beyond these few birds and mammals. A leg-stretching, short walk away from the road reveals the subtle richness of lifeforms found in this open land.

On a warm, sunny day at the height of spring, the first signs of life are usually audible ones. Birds call from the surrounding sea of sagebrush: the twitterings of the sage sparrow, the flute-like melody of a western meadowlark on a weathered fence post, a series of warblings from a sage thrasher perched atop a bush, and the high-pitched call of the horned lark. Insects add a busy undertone of sound; the murmuring drone of bees, the intensely high-pitched buzz of a cicada and the sudden clicking flight of startled grasshoppers.

The observant hiker may see the small sagebrush lizard darting among the bushes,or the short-horned lizard, a pygmy-sized member of the misnamed "horny toad" group. In rocky areas, sun-loving reptiles include the western fence lizard, side-blotched lizard and a sleek snake that preys upon them, the racer. Eye-catching butterflies of many patterns and colors fly among the spring wildflowers, while legions of busy ants radiate from their swarming anthills.

Ground-dwelling squirrels scurry about the sagebrush plains: the petite least chipmunk, the more moderately-sized Townsend ground squirrel and, from the top of rock outcrops, the large, bulky yellow-bellied marmot (popularly known as the rockchuck).

Farther from the road, more wary wildlife demands quiet, slow movements, patience and, sometimes, field glasses.

The pronghorn antelope epitomizes the freedom of the prairie. Not true antelopes, these alert animals rely on speed as their defense, sometimes exceeding 40 miles per hour for short distances. However, pronghorns are extremely curious and will invariably stop to look back after an initial run puts them at a more comfortable distance from a disturbance.

Just as the pronghorn represents freedom on the run, the prairie falcon symbolizes the unrestrained liberty of the vaulted desert skies. Superbly designed for speed, this streamlined bird of prey may exceed 100 miles per hour when it plunges like a diving rocket to capture other flying birds for food. Prairie falcons hunt the open

Above: *Magpie.* GEORGE WUERTHNER
Left: *Yellow-bellied marmot on alert.*
CHRIS LUNESKI

21

gnomes conducting serious discussions. Burrowing owls use an excellent imitation of a rattlesnake's buzz to scare enemies away from the nest.

In the lower, true desert basins and sedimentary "badlands" of Southeastern Oregon, a variety of animals adapted to extreme aridity reach the northern extents of their ranges in western North America. Good examples are reptiles especially suited to these sunny, dry habitats. Moving about on sandy areas between the greasewood, saltbush and other desert shrubs are large desert lizards typical of the Great Basin: the leopard lizard, western whiptail and desert horned lizard. On sandy hillsides among scattered rocks scampers Oregon's largest lizard, the desert collared lizard, which often attains a total length of 13″. Oregon's rarest snake also occurs in these remote basins and canyons, the little, burrowing ground snake with its bright orange and black markings.

Other animals that flourish in Oregon only in these deserts include the attractively marked black-throated sparrow, white-tailed antelope ground squirrel, Richardson's ground squirrel and the little kit fox with its large, alert ears. Hiding under rocks, a host of arachnids (popularly and collectively referred to as "creepy-crawly critters") ranges from scorpions and centipedes to spiders, with the four-inch-long, greenish-yellow giant hairy scorpion the most notable.

Surprisingly, several species of fish are endemic to the dry country of Southeastern Oregon. Trapped in landlocked desert basins as large glacial reservoirs receded, leaving behind only shallow alkaline lakes and small streams, the Alvord cutthroat, redband trout and Alvord chub inhabit no other waters in the world.

As the desert sun sinks low, a number of other animals become active, often through the entire night. Daytime temperatures are too high during the desert summers for many species. Snakes such as the gopher snake (also called the bull snake) and western rattlesnake emerge in the evening from their cool, daytime retreats in rodent burrows and deep rock crevices. With darkness, bats of several species begin their nightly pursuit of winged insects, while the ghostly white form of the barn owl's silent flight betrays its search for nocturnal rodents.

After sunset, the desert comes alive with the hurry-scurry of countless small mice and rats. Great Basin pocket mice, sagebrush voles, northern grasshopper mice, dark kangaroo mice, western harvest mice and deer mice comprise this midnight army of rodents. Two

rangelands as well as rocky canyons and mountain cliffs, where they lay their eggs on high, bare clefts of precipices.

Perhaps no other animal is so closely intertwined with the sagebrush steppe habitat as the sage grouse. The males of this species perform an annual spring mating ritual for their females, always using the same sagebrush-enshrouded ancestral strutting grounds *(leks)*. These High Desert dandies enact a complicated courtship performance that entails repeated strutting, tail-fanning, wing-arching and popping sounds made by rapidly enlarging and deflating air sacks on the bird's breast.

An interesting relationship exists between the badger, which excavates roomy burrows with its powerfully clawed forelimbs, and the burrowing owl, which often appropriates abandoned badger homes for nests. Although owls generally are active at night, burrowing owls often appear at the entrances of these burrows during daylight hours—especially the young, which gather at their nest entrances like groups of little, knock-kneed

species of gentle-natured kangaroo rats (Ord's and chisel-toothed) hop through the sagebrush as they forage in the darkness, stuffing their cheek pouches with seeds. Another nighttime prowler, the desert wood rat, continues to earn an infamous place in desert lore as the thieving pack rat. These rodents have a strong attraction for small, shiny objects in human camps and cabins, and hoarding their loot in nests of sticks.

No other nocturnal animal gives a voice to the loneliness and expanse of the desert better than the coyote. Anyone who has sat by a sagebrush campfire at night and listened to its yipping howl sensed something of the soul of this harsh land. The coyote personifies the myth, the very essence of the arid American West. Both loved and hated by mankind, the coyote's adaptability and resourcefulness earn it the respect of friend and foe alike. These wily canines prowl throughout much of Oregon, but they seem most at home on the sagebrush plains.

The marshlands of the High Desert act like magnets to draw waterfowl. Densely vegetated aquatic areas like Malheur and Klamath lakes are extremely rich, life-supporting ecosystems with incredible concentrations of wildlife. These basin marshes of Eastern Oregon, located on the Pacific Flyway, attract spectacular numbers of migratory birds during spring and autumn.

At slightly higher elevations, the western juniper belt supports a large variety of birdlife. The black-billed magpie builds its stick nests here, while pinyon jays, Townsend's solitaires and California quail move through the fragrant trees. The rocky canyons also shelter their own special types of wildlife, such as the canyon wren voicing its distinctive, descending call, which fades away as if it were falling from a cliff.

Higher still, the large ponderosa pine forests support several species of squirrels, such as the yellow pine chipmunk and the larger golden-mantled ground squirrel, which looks as though it belongs in a Disney animated movie. Tree squirrels are represented in the daytime by the active red squirrel (sometimes called the pine squirrel), while the night shift enlists the northern flying squirrel, with its folds of skin at its sides for gliding from tree to tree.

Other forest mammals common in the mountainous country of Northeastern and Central Oregon are the black bear, Rocky Mountain elk, porcupine, red and gray fox, pine marten, mink and short-tailed and long-tailed weasels. The wolverine is extremely rare, sighted only in

Above: *Coyote.*
NEAL & MARY JANE MISHLER
Left: *Northern Pacific rattlesnake.*
ALAN D. ST. JOHN

Bighorn sheep in Leslie Gulch, Owyhee River Canyon. ALAN D. ST. JOHN

rubber boa. Cold, rocky streams in the Wallowa Mountains are inhabited by a diminutive amphibian known as the tailed frog, the "tail" being a reproductive appendage found only on the males of this peculiar species.

Higher yet, the snowy white mountain goat lives among the rocky crags of the Wallowa and Elkhorn mountains. These sure-footed mountaineers are not native Oregonians, having been introduced some years ago. Rockslides near timberline house a small mammal known as the pika (pronounced "peeka" here). Hikers will hear this Guinea-pig–like creature's characteristic "screech-screech" warning cry as it scampers between rock crevices. Pikas do not hibernate through the long, brutal alpine winters; instead, they survive on caches of dried "hay" they have stored in passages under boulders.

No account of forest wildlife would be complete without mention of a most distinctive bird. Anyone who spends time exploring along a mountain stream may be surprised to see a small, gray, wren-like bird hop from a rock into the rushing waters and walk about on the stream-bottom. This is the dipper (sometimes called the water ouzel). These robin-sized birds are the constant companions of the forest water courses, whose waters they never leave, bobbing up and down on spray-soaked rocks, their ringing, bubbling song being heard summer through winter.

Several animals typical of the wooded western portions of the state also extend their ranges into Central Oregon along the eastern flanks of the Cascades: the western gray squirrel, Douglas tree squirrel, California ground squirrel, spotted owl, Pacific giant salamander, alligator lizard and ringneck snake.

Other species have adapted successfully throughout most of Eastern Oregon. The mule deer, bobcat, mountain lion, striped and spotted skunks, deer mouse, robin and common garter snake thrive almost everywhere east of the Cascades. River otters, muskrats and beavers inhabit most suitable aquatic habitats. Even moisture-requiring amphibians, such as the Pacific tree frog and western toad, have adapted throughout Eastern Oregon's dry climate. And the Great Basin spadefoot toad is particularly suited to aridity. Using small, sharp-edged nubbins on its feet, this little amphibian burrows into the ground, often remaining buried for long dry periods. After seasonal rains, spadefoots emerge to quickly mate and lay eggs in temporary rainpools, where the eggs and resulting tadpoles transform rapidly.

more remote areas. The dainty whitetail deer is not widespread, found only in the wooded foothills and canyons of Northeastern Oregon.

Mountain birds include the Steller's jay, gray jay, Clark's nutcracker, mountain chickadee, several species of hummingbirds, pileated woodpecker, mountain bluebird, western tanager, mountain quail and ruffed and blue grouse. The sleek Cooper's and sharp-shinned hawks and the uncommon northern goshawk hunt these coniferous woods. Around lakes, the fish-catching osprey and stately bald eagle perch on snags at the water's edge. At night, these forests echo with the bass hooting of the great horned owl and the trilling whistle of the little screech owl. The rare great gray owl sends its deep, booming "whoos" into densely timbered sections.

Under moist, rotting logs on the shadowy forest floor live small, secretive creatures, such as the long-toed salamander and an unusual, stubby little snake called the

Top left: *California quail.* RON SPOMER
Above: *Mountain goat.*
GEORGE WUERTHNER
Far left: *Badger.* DAN DAVIDSON
Left: *Desert collared lizard.*
ALAN D. ST. JOHN

Oregon's rivers are famous for their trout and other game fish, especially steelhead and salmon. However, within the last century native populations have declined due to human pressures and competition from introduced, non-native fish. Many conservation groups now are questioning Oregon's annual stocking of streams with hatchery-raised fish and are calling for greater protection and enhancement of wild native species.

Much of Eastern Oregon seems deceptively wild and remote, uninfluenced by human civilization. The adverse, long-term effects of heavy grazing, instances of improper logging practices, pesticide pollution, competitive non-native species, abuse of streamside riparian habitats, encroachment of access roads into the last retreats of shy wildlife, overhunting and many other pressures have taken their collective toll over the past century. Wolves and grizzly bears could not fit into man's plans for the land and were exterminated in Oregon decades ago. The lynx, too, disappeared.

However, Oregon has learned important wildlife management lessons from its past mistakes. As a result, a strong environmental protection ethic has evolved within the state's outdoor-oriented population. The Oregon Department of Fish and Wildlife's progressive fish, game and non-game management programs complement a fine network of wildlife refuges managed by the state, U.S. government and non-profit conservation organizations such as the Nature Conservancy. Several animals exterminated in the past have been successfully reintroduced: most notably bighorn sheep, which are again prospering in several locations of Eastern Oregon's rocky ranges.

As more people discover the outdoor opportunities available in this ruggedly beautiful country east of the Cascades, greater stresses threaten the land's plant communities and native wildlife. Balancing the demands of cattle ranching, logging, hunting, fishing and outdoor recreation with adequate protection for the region's natural environment will become more and more difficult. Wise decisions now will formulate a true "multiple-use" land management program for Eastern Oregon's future.

Above: *A bull elk marshals his harem during fall rut.* JERRY LONG
Right: *Golden-mantled ground squirrel.* NEAL & MARY JANE MISHLER

Clockwise from upper right:
Wild chinook salmon using a fish ladder to cross McNary Dam. BRYAN PETERSON
Biologists attach a radio collar to this coyote for monitoring. JANIS MIGLAVS
Fox squirrel. NEAL & MARY JANE MISHLER
Canada geese swimming in autumn reflections near Bend. STEVE ANTELL

PART II

Central Oregon

Above: Ponderosa pine logging in the Ochoco Mountains. DAVID JENSEN *Right: The Three Sisters.* JIM ROMO
Facing page, top: Crooked River in Smith Rocks State Park. LARRY ULRICH
Bottom: A hard day's work in Central Oregon still is just that. BRYAN PETERSON
Right: Mill Creek drains the luxuriant Mill Creek Wilderness in Ochoco National Forest. LARRY ULRICH

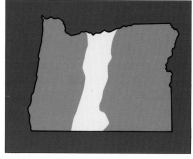

From Sagebrush Sandals to Ski Boots

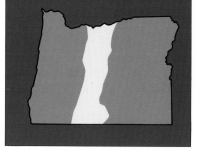

Right: *Pines barely shelter this weathered outbuilding in the Upper Klamath Basin.* JEFF GNASS

It will be seen that the Deschutes Valley is mostly a barren region, furrowed by immense canyons, and offering very few inducements to settlers. Its few fertile spots, excepting those in the immediate vicinity of The Dalles, are separated from the rest of the world by almost impassable barriers and nature seems to have guaranteed it forever to the wandering savage and the lonely seeker after the wild and sublime in natural scenery.

Lt. Henry L. Abbot, in his report
of an 1855 pioneer horseback survey
of possible railroad routes
into Central Oregon

The overwhelming impact of the wild and harsh character of Central Oregon on early white explorers emerges in journal entries such as Lieutenant Abbot's. If such dramatic pronouncements seem humorous compared with the region's present-day highways, railroads, farmlands and modern cities, we must reflect upon the times in which they were written.

In the early 1800s the only way to reach Oregon's largely unexplored interior plateau was by lengthy, arduous travel, either by foot or horseback. No clearly marked trails or roads led the way into this frontier and its awesomely deep canyons were without bridges. Away from river courses, locating water was a dangerous problem in this dry land. Much of the food on these long marches came from hunting and some local Indian tribes were hostile toward strange, light-skinned invaders.

Even today, Central Oregon's grand scenery can overwhelm the senses—one reason this area is fast becoming Oregon's premier outdoor recreation mecca. And despite the civilizing influences of the 20th century, large portions of the region still retain a comparatively wild, Old West flavor.

Because of its geographical location at the very heart of the state, Central Oregon has a remarkable amalgamation of nearly all the features found east of the Cascades. And, influences of Western Oregon spill over the forested Cascades and also contribute to Central Oregon's makeup.

Dominating Central Oregon, the imposing volcanic peaks of the snowy High Cascade Crest define the western skyline. On the eastern borders of the northern portion of the region are the pine-clad Ochoco Mountains, a western extension of the Blue Mountains. The southern half of Central Oregon bounds the western edge of the arid Great Basin Desert. And within these natural perimeters, Central Oregon gathers a stunning variety of topographic features that include broad forests of ponderosa pines; dry, open juniper woodlands; sagebrush High Desert; deep, rocky gorges; snow-fed, rushing rivers and streams; cascading waterfalls; crystal-clear mountain lakes; basin lakes and marshes; grassy hillsides scattered with oak trees; large, green meadows; moonscape lava fields; lava caves; a huge volcanic depression a mile wide; a gigantic, fortress-like rock monolith; rainbow-colored desert hills; and an immense volcanic mountain crater that cradles two sky-blue lakes.

Of course, early white explorers were not the first to gaze upon these natural wonders. Long, long before, predating more recent Native American tribes by unknown numbers of generations, Central Oregon's true first explorers encountered this land.

No one knows for certain just who these ancient ones were. Evidence indicates that they were small, wandering bands of aboriginal, ice age hunter-gatherers, probably of Asian origin, who slowly drifted from the far north. Their descendants can be traced through the modern Canadian Indians and Arctic Eskimos. These prehistoric ancestors of all North and South American native tribes crossed a then-exposed land bridge between what are now Russia and Alaska and unwittingly discovered a

huge new continent. Hardy people, they were following and hunting Pleistocene animals, including such exotic, now-extinct food sources as woolly mammoths.

Humans are thought to have arrived in Oregon some 14,000 to 15,000 years ago. The oldest human artifacts unearthed east of the Cascades in this state are those from Fort Rock Cave in northern Lake County. There, in what is now a dry, sandy High Desert basin, archaeologists found 9,000-year-old woven sagebrush sandals, basketry, matting, scrapers, knives, stone awls and animal bones, along with projectile points carbon dated at 13,500 years. Stone weights used on nets for capturing water fowl indicate that Fort Rock Valley contained a lake at that time.

Whitebark pines defy a lava flow within sight of the Three Sisters and the Cascade Range.
GEORGE WUERTHNER

Excavations at Cow Cave Butte, also called Fort Rock Cave, revealed 9,000-year-old sagebrush sandals once worn by Indians where the High Desert now dominates Lake County. ALAN D. ST. JOHN

As Central Oregon's climate gradually became drier and the lakes receded and vanished, the inhabitants shifted to a broader spectrum of resources. These bands of First Americans settled into various sections of the region and lived there for generation after generation, their ways of life eventually merging with the land around them. Food-gathering, fishing, hunting, clothing, shelter, social customs, songs, ceremonies, religions and myths all harmonized in an earthy, practical way deeply based in these peoples' spiritual life. Each tribe's culture reflected the ebb and flow of seasons, and cycles in the natural world around it. There were much trading and other interaction between the various plateau tribes east of the Cascades, and with coastal groups as well.

When the first white trappers arrived in Central Oregon in the early 1800s, they found colorful groups of people with evocative names: Wasco, Wyam, Tygh, Tenino, Paiute and Klamath. Needless to say, the meeting of entirely different cultures and races produced quite a shock. Some tribes welcomed the pale-skinned explorers into their land; others resented the intrusion and tried to discourage the invaders. Such was the continuation of a sad and regretfully shameful period in our nation's history of tribal land loss and devastation of native cultures from the east coast westward. Beginning with the native peoples' being misnamed as "Indians," the misunderstandings by whites have continued to the present day.

At the beginning of the 19th century, the only white settlements in the Oregon Territory were fur company outposts, most established by the famed Hudson's Bay Company. These were located in what is now the Portland/Vancouver area and father inland along the mighty Columbia River. Interior Central Oregon was largely ignored until 1825 to 1827, when Peter Skene Ogden, representing the Hudson's Bay Company, led two exploratory expeditions up the Deschutes River into this high, wild country east of the Cascades. His harrowing treks, the parties composed of hardy, outdoors-loving trappers, mountain men and Indian guides, tested even these tough men. During the first journey, horses were lost crossing of the swollen Deschutes, the expedition spent a grim winter trapping and exploring the mountains, and finally they butchered some of their remaining horses to escape starvation. During the second trip, despite attackes by hostile Indians and still more drowned horses, Ogden and his party accomplished much in the way of exploration. They were among the first whites to see and describe such Eastern Oregon features as the Malheur-Harney region, the Klamath Basin, and the Paulina Mountains' huge crater containing two lakes. The group even ventured into Northern California, discovering and naming Mt. Shasta.

Following Ogden's example, other explorers, such as John Work and Nathaniel J. Wyeth, investigated the Central Oregon area. Wyeth, a trapper and trader, led the first probe by whites into what is now the Bend area, then continued on into the upper Deschutes drainage.

However, the best-known expedition through Central Oregon was led by colorful John C. Frémont, accompanied by the equally colorful scout Kit Carson, and guided by a Wasco Indian, Billy Chinook. Frémont, then a young lieutenant with the Topographic Engineers of the U.S. Army, was rather ambitiously assigned to "explore the West." With a number of men under his command, and a cannon to assure protection from hostile Indians, Frémont left The Dalles on November 25, 1843, and progressed south, up the Deschutes River, to the Klamath area of South-Central Oregon. From there, the party moved eastward into forested mountains, weathering a bitterly cold snowstorm. When the struggling group at last broke out of the trees onto the top of a high escarpment, they were astonished at the view that spread before them. Far below the vertical dropoff, sunshine bathed a large basin valley and its grass-edged lake. The dramatic contrast in this scene prompted Frémont to christen the stormy rim-top on which they stood Winter Ridge and the attractive water below, Summer Lake. The Frémont expedition continued eastward, on through Southeastern Oregon, and then south into California.

Most early settlers who crossed the continent in wagon trains on the Oregon Trail bypassed interior Central Oregon. They instead followed the Columbia River to their goal, the fertile green Willamette Valley. However, several adventurous caravans abandoned the main route at the Snake River and crossed the middle of the state through the sagebrush-covered High Desert and the southern slopes of the Blue Mountains. These pioneer settlers often bisected the trails of those earlier pathfinders—Frémont, Work and Wyeth.

Of these inland Oregon wagon trains, the first and most famous caravan to try this route, which became known later as the Blue Bucket Train. Led by Stephen Meek, the band of 800 people and 200 wagons ventured across the Oregon High Desert in 1845, attempting to navigate this trailless, unknown expanse. Soon lost, a number of the immigrants died of dehydration and from drinking alkali water. After moving northwest to reach the Crooked River in the area of present-day Prineville, they finally met a rescue group from The Dalles, alerted by Meek and another train member who had ridden ahead. The rescuers aided and guided the stricken caravan to The Dalles. Despite this group's hardships, other wagon trains soon followed through the desert on what became known as the Meek Cutoff.

How the "Blue Bucket" appellation became attached to this group has become a venerable legend of the Old West. As one verson of the story goes, while camped at a stream some children collected water in a blue bucket. Later, after the wagon train had moved some distance, someone noticed gold nuggets in the bottom of the bucket. Subsequently, after the rescued train reached its destination, members tried unsuccessfully to retrace their route and find the nugget-bearing stream. And for more than a hundred years other gold seekers, too, have tried in vain to relocate the source of the famous blue-bucket nuggets.

Despite that disastrous first crossing of interior Oregon, other wagon trains soon followed their tracks across the desert sands. Paiute Indians massacred one party near

The Columbia River near Biggs and Miller Island. DAVID JENSEN

the Snake River. Another lost its way in the desert: a trail of discarded furniture and belongings marked this erratic, desperate journey as drivers lightened the wagons for their dehydrated beasts. But regardless of hardships and suffering, determined pioneers could not be dissuaded from this perilous trek. The opening of Barlow Pass over the Cascades near Mt. Hood eliminated the need for a harrowing float trip through the Columbia River Gorge to the Willamette Valley. Thus, the short-cut across Oregon's central plateau became even more attractive to weary travelers on the long Oregon Trail. Guided by the snow-capped beacons of the Cascade peaks in the heat-shimmering distance, the wagon trains kept coming across the High Desert.

Although the promised land of mild climate and rich soils—the Willamette Valley—was their goal, many of these first settlers remembered grassy meadows along the Crooked River and the ponderosa pine forests edging the rushing Deschutes River and returned in later years. Its first white residents began to settle Central Oregon, but not without risks.

Typical Stage of Central Oregon

B.B. Bakowski of Bend offered this picture of a Central Oregon stagecoach in the summer of 1911. NEG. NO. 6548, OREGON HISTORICAL SOCIETY

rier to separate whites and Native Americans, hoping to prevent conflicts between the two races. Settlers were forbidden to homestead east of the mountains in the interior of Oregon. Soon, however, this edict became extremely difficult to enforce and the order was revoked.

Several U.S. Army forts had been established in Eastern Oregon by this time. At one of these, Fort Klamath in South-Central Oregon, an 1864 peace meeting gathered white officials and representatives of Oregon's dissatisfied Indian tribes. Chief Paulina and his band of Northern Paiutes did not attend, however, foreshadowing one of Eastern Oregon's bloodiest chapters in Native American resistance against white intrusion.

Although the Homestead Act of 1862 offered lands for settlement in the West, few white settlers yet had come to the wild and remote interior of Oregon. There were no communities of any kind and the only "road" ran south from The Dalles, crossed the Deschutes at Sherars Bridge, and progressed easterly to the gold fields in the Blue Mountains of Northeastern Oregon. With the discovery of gold there in 1861, the need to transport supplies and passengers had prompted the formation of a regularly-running stagecoach line on this route by 1864. For several years, Paulina burned and pillaged way stations and attacked travelers along this road. No settler in the area believed his home or livestock safe. On one notable occasion, Paiutes attacked Henry Wheeler, owner of the stage lines, near the present site of Mitchell. His one passenger kept the attackers at bay with rifle shots while Wheeler unhitched the stage and the men escaped on the horses. Wheeler was shot through the cheeks, the bullet passing through his mouth without doing serious damage. The Indians destroyed the stage and found $10,000 in currency amongst the cargo, but they threw the "worthless paper" into the sagebrush.

To protect settlers and miners, the army eventually established small, manned outposts at several localities in Eastern Oregon. In the central area of the state, Camp Polk was set along Squaw Creek, near the present location of Sisters. Still, continued skirmishes between soldiers and Paulina's raiders in the Crooked River/Ochoco area inflicted a number of casualties on both sides.

Not even aid from from friendly Warm Springs Indians enabled the army to stop Paulina. Ironically, it was simply a rancher, Howard Maupin, accompanied by three other settlers, who finally ended Paulina's renegade career on April 25, 1867. After Paulina's band had stolen cattle from the Andrew Clarno ranch, the four men

Most Native American tribes of Eastern Oregon proved friendly to white settlers, but others refused to give up their traditional homelands without a fight.

In 1855, the Wasco tribe and another large tribe consisting of four Sahaptin-speaking bands (the Wyam, Tenino, Tygh and John Day) were persuaded to give up 10 million acres of their combined traditional tribal lands along the mid-Columbia River and the lower Deschutes to the U.S. government. In return, they received the equivalent of $150,000 in goods and promised services. They were moved to a 578,000-acre southerly section of their territory along the Deschutes River, where Northern Paiutes later were also required to settle. Thus, the Warm Springs Indian Reservation opened most of North-Central Oregon's finest lands to white settlement. A Klamath Reservation established in South-Central Oregon at about the same time also freed Indian lands for settlement.

For two years following this Indian relocation, the U.S. Army attempted to use the Cascade Mountains as a bar-

tracked the cattle and thieves through an entire night. They discovered the Indians the following morning in a rock-rimmed basin along Trout Creek, north of the present-day site of Prineville. Hiding in the rocks, the ranchers opened fire on the unsuspecting Paiutes, and Maupin reportedly shot and killed the Chief Paulina. Although occasional Indian attacks followed Paulina's death, by the early 1870s, peace between whites and Indians generally prevailed.

The influx of new settlers to Central Oregon then accelerated greatly, spurred by the Homestead Act, which allowed a U.S. citizen to acquire 160 acres of government land for a small fee and a few minimum occupancy requirements.

As more families arrived, organized communities appeared. The first school in Central Oregon, a one-room, rough-hewn structure, was built in 1868 along Mill Creek in the foothills of the Ochoco Mountains. More schools followed throughout the area, supplemented by rustic churches. A few miles down Ochoco Creek from the Mill Creek school, Barney Prine and his family established a store at their ranch in the wild rye-grass meadows. These large, grassy flats invited tired travelers along the stage route and by 1877 other homes, a livery stable, hotel and a Baptist Church had sprung up. Interior Oregon had its first true town, Prineville. Other small villages followed, including Ashwood, Antelope and Mitchell, often little more than stage stops, possibly with post offices. Camp Polk, no longer a military base, picked up in 1888 and moved its post office to the new hamlet of Sisters, three miles to the west. Other communities to the south formed toward the end of the century: La Pine, Silver Lake, Lakeview and Klamath Falls.

Interestingly, Bend, which eventually became the largest city in Eastern Oregon, was one of the later towns to develop, as were Redmond and Madras. In the meantime, Prineville became a thriving city and the hub of the region for many years. This bustling town, along with the ranches of the area that it served, provided a background for many "wild west"-style occurrences that seem to be perfect for the old "Gunsmoke" television series. In fact, local people called their region "the West's last frontier," and with good reason.

For a period of about two years (1882-1884), before organized law enforcement protected this remote area, a group of vigilantes held sway with their own interpretation of law and order. With no court system to slow the process of dealing with supposed lawbreakers, the vig-

Above: *Pioneer ranch buildings stand like monuments to gutsy settlers near Ukiah, Umatilla County.* JEFF GNASS
Left: *Mt. Hood crowns this view of a picturesque Wasco County cemetery.* DAVID JENSEN

ilantes handled situations quickly, usually with a six-shooter or lynching rope slung over a convenient juniper limb. When, after a property dispute, two ranchers were found shot to death, these masked vigilantes efficiently dealt retribution to the two accused murderers. They forced their way into the town's hotel, where one suspect was being held for trial in The Dalles, and killed him with pistol shots. The other alleged killer, not arrested because of lack of evidence, was captured by the vigilantes, dragged behind a horse down the dusty main street, and hanged from a bridge at the edge of town. Posing as a stockmen's organization, these masked law-enforcers anonymously ruled the area, punishing whatever they judged to be infractions with shootings, lynchings and mysterious disappearances. Tiring of this tyrannical rule, another (and larger) group of respected men, who wished to bring organized law to the Prineville district, banded together as a strong militia and publicly opposed the vigilantes. To demonstrate their serious intentions, the group of about 75 men rode down the main street of town fully armed. Apparently, this display had its desired effect: soon afterward the masked vigilantes disbanded and residents elected a town marshal and deputy.

Unfortunately, gunfire and bloodshed continued in Central Oregon. Trouble was brewing out on the sagebrush rangelands in the form of a range war. Since the late 1860s, enterprising men had been building cattle ranches in Central Oregon until some had become "cattle empires," a few claiming millions of acres. Sheep were also grazing in the region—one operation, the famous Hays Creek Ranch, near Madras, attained the same super size as the big cattle ranches.

Inevitably, grazing disputes erupted between sheep and cattle ranchers forced to share the open range. Some of the worst clashes flared into all-out range wars around the turn of the century. One group of cattlemen, wishing to rid the range of competing sheep, organized themselves as the "Crook County Sheep Shooting Association," named after their local county. Their tactics were simple: upon finding a sheepherder using "their" range, the cattlemen donned masks, captured the herder at gunpoint, blindfolded him and tied him to tree. The sheep-shooters then proceeded to live up to their name, shooting every wooly animal. In 1903, one of the largest of these shootings occurred at Benjamin Lake on the High Desert east of Bend, destroying more than 2,400 sheep. Government intervention finally settled the dispute by allotting and issuing permits for separate, designated grazing areas.

Above: A white-frame church building at Antelope embodies the practical, resolute spirit that built Central Oregon. BILL STORMONT
Right: In Shaniko, a friendly stagecoach driver invites visitors to ride into the past. JANIS MIGLAVS

While Prineville endured its turbulent growing pains, 35 miles to the southwest a small community quietly emerged. In 1879, John Y. Todd started a cattle ranch along the Deschutes River where the water makes a large bend. This location at the edge of the Cascade Mountains was well known to many generations of Indians who had camped there and, later, to dusty wagon trains coming off the High Desert to the east. The attractive, park-like setting of big ponderosa pines along the winding river, grassy glades, views of the snowy Cascade peaks to the west, and plentiful fish and game, made this a natural stopping place. Early travelers named the site "Farewell Bend" because the old stage road left the river behind at this point and stretched into dry, open country.

Other settlers soon built homes near Todd's Farewell Bend Ranch and the little village in the pines began to grow. By 1886, a post office opened and postal authorities shortened the town's name to Bend. In June of 1900, Alexander M. Drake, a wealthy entrepreneur and fishing enthusiast from the Midwest, camped at Bend with his wife and a guide. Besides being on vacation, Drake was looking for new business possibilities and a new place to live. He liked what he saw, decided to stay, and by autumn was building a large log home by this wide bend in the Deschutes River.

Undoubtedly, no other person exerted such influence upon the initial growth of Bend and the surrounding Deschutes Valley. Drake realized the immense possibilities of the abundant waters of the Deschutes for irrigation and, with his planning and financial backing, three Bend pumping plants soon delivered water to the surrounding dry soil. Within the next several years, a network of irrigation canals began to spread outward into the open sagebrush and juniper country. As more and more land was cleared, plowed and irrigated, word spread quickly throughout the nation of the opportunities available in the Bend area. A new influx of settlers swelled the population of Oregon's sunny heartland.

Sixteen miles to the north of Bend, the community of Redmond sprouted in 1905 as formerly dry rangelands gradually were nourished into green croplands and pastures. The Redmond area eventually became one of the largest sections of irrigated land in the Pacific Northwest and the agricultural hub of Central Oregon. Twenty-six miles to the north, Madras also took shape. Still farther to the north, a railroad from The Dalles reached south to the little, high-plains town of Shaniko in the heart of

An abandoned miner's cabin perches stubbornly on a slope near Clarno, in the John Day River Canyon of Wheeler County.
ALAN D. ST. JOHN

sheep country, and Shaniko quickly became one of the largest wool-shipping centers in the world. Central Oregon was prospering.

Unfortunately, opportunity also brought tragedy. The federal government stimulated immigration with its 1909 Revised Homestead Act, which granted settlers 320 acres of land for a $10.00 fee and required only that they move onto the land within six months after filing and "improve" their claim within five years. Approximately one and a half million acres of arid High Desert land southeast of Bend was opened for homesteading. For a fee, unscrupulous real estate developers and "locaters" aided hopeful young families to find their bit of Uncle Sam's free land. Many of these naive people, fresh from eastern cities, had never seen such wild deserts and mountains. Rumors of future irrigation canals and a railroad line into the High Desert never came true, and new settlers soon discovered that it was difficult to grow even a potato in the higher-elevation, more arid climate. Within a few dry years, most families left, disillusioned and ex-

Above: By the first decade of this century, irrigation began to radiate from Bend (seen here in 1910) and nourish, besides crops, the economic and population growth of the entire region. COLLECTION OF DON FRANKS
Right: The Deschutes River cuts through a lava flow at Dillon Falls. LINDA ROBINSON
Facing page: Summer flowers bloom around Russell Lake in Mt. Jefferson Park. LARRY GEDDIS

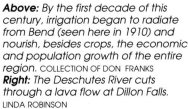

hausted, their savings gone. Today, lonely desert winds moan in the cracks in these disintegrating family homes while sifting desert sands bury abandoned dreams.

While the High Desert homesteaders were experiencing failure, the young city of Bend was prospering. In 1903, the *Bend Bulletin* newspaper began in a log cabin by the river. By 1904, the town was connected to the outside world by telephone and the first automobile chugged down its dusty main street. An "Auto Stage," the first inter-city bus in the U.S., began shuttling passengers over a primitive road between Bend and the rail terminus at Shaniko. Gas street lights, installed in 1907, had been converted by 1910 to electricity thanks to a small power dam built across the river. The long-awaited railroad line finally reached Bend in 1911, and with this transportation connection the city evolved from an agricultural town into a mill town. Two large commercial lumber mills, constructed in 1916, served logging railroads penetrating vast stands of pines outside of the city.

Besides a new, booming forest products industry, Bend confronted another major change 1916. Huge Crook

County, which had originally included most of the central portion of Oregon, was subdivided and Bend became the county seat of the new Deschutes County. By this time, Bend was clearly the leader of growing Central Oregon communities and soon became the largest population center of the entire Eastern Oregon region. In later years, with improved transportation and modern highway systems, tourism and outdoor recreation added new resources to the area's rich assets. With the opening of a new ski development on Mt. Bachelor in 1958, Bend developed into one of the Pacific Northwest's most popular ski and resort destinations.

The span of fewer than 100 years had belied Henry Abbot's prediction that the remote wilderness he explored in 1855 never would be civilized.

Railroad Wars

Above: *Pressure gauge of a steam locomotive.* DAN DAVIDSON
Right: *Workmen climb a rope ladder for a day's work building the Oregon Trunk Railroad bridge over the Crooked River in 1911.* NEG. 9967, OREGON HISTORICAL SOCIETY
Top right: *The bridge itself takes shape, 320 feet above the river.* NEG. 21959, OREGON HISTORICAL SOCIETY

From 1909 to 1911, one of the most dramatic struggles in the West's saga of pioneer railroad expansion took place in Central Oregon. For two years, the construction crews of two of the nation's most powerful railroad magnates, James J. Hill of the Great Northern Railroad, and Edward H. Harriman of the Union Pacific, fought their way up opposite sides of the Deschutes River Canyon, from the Columbia River to Bend.

One lucrative goal spurred this competition: the vast, stands of ponderosa pine that bordered the young town of Bend. A long-awaited railroad connection to this remote community promised transportation for this wealth of timber to the markets of the outside world. Large Minnesota lumber firms already had made long-range plans for the area. Both Hill and Harriman knew the railroad company that arrived at Bend first would win the shipping contracts. The race was on.

More than just a race, the long, grueling battle between these two tycoons' rowdy work crews demanded stamina and engineering skill. As early as 1855, the government's Pacific Railroad Survey had explored this frontier and reported that the deep, rugged gorges of this inhospitable land presented inaccessible barriers. It concluded that building a railroad up the Deschutes River was impossible.

Hill's Great Northern project was the Oregon Trunk Line, while Harriman's Union Pacific project was the DesChutes Railroad. Before actual construction began, both companies undertook various legal maneuvers and bought stock to acquire important holdings and block each other. Hill scored an important coup when he obtained a strategic site for a railroad crossing on a major Deschutes tributary, the Crooked River.

Before legal surveys could be fully completed, both crews set up camps at locations along the canyon, the DesChutes Railroad taking the east bank of the river while the Oregon Trunk Line claimed the west side. Hill's men acquired a head start by beginning work under the cover of darkness during the night of July 26, 1909. The following morning, the Harriman crew discovered that their wagon road for transporting supplies had been sabotaged and was impassable. The no-holds-barred battle had begun in earnest.

Through that first hot summer's work, each side used many tactics to discourage and slow the opponent's progress. Periodically, several men would swim across the river at night, find the other crew's store of blasting powder and explode the entire supply. At other times shooting occurred, crews taking potshots at each other across the canyon. No one was actually hit, but the shootings did intimidate would-be workers.

Within a few months, as autumn's cooler weather arrived, the first heat of battle subsided. The companies now fully concentrated on the back-breaking work of blasting, digging, hauling and clearing a railroad bed up both sides of the rocky gorge. Thousands of men labored with hand tools and wheelbarrows and laid track for two years, through summer heat and winter snow.

This warring, parallel contest raged on up the Deschutes until both lines converged near the small community of Metolius on the plateau above the east rim. After an intense struggle in the courts, a truce was called. One line, jointly used, would be completed by Hill's construction crew.

After a total cost of $25 million, James J. Hill drove in a final spike made of solid gold at the railroad's terminus in Bend on October 5, 1911. More than 2,000 celebrants watched the ceremony that marked the end of this unusual railroad war.

By 1928, tracks had been extended south to connect with the Western Pacific line in California. To the east, Prineville needed its own connecting railroad, as it too had large timber resources in the Ochoco Mountains. In 1918, a line constructed by the city itself extended west down the Crooked River to connect the north-south line along the Deschutes. This unique railroad is still city-owned and -operated.

Above and left: The Sumpter Valley Railroad near Sumpter still attracts visitors. STEVE TERRILL

41

The Middle Ground: High Tech Meets Old West

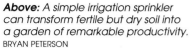

Above: *A simple irrigation sprinkler can transform fertile but dry soil into a garden of remarkable productivity.* BRYAN PETERSON

Right: *Near its headwaters, the lovely Deschutes River reflects Mt. Bachelor.* LINDA ROBINSON

Modern Central Oregon occupies a unique, dynamic equilibrium between the wild and civilized, the natural and the developed. Both its geographic location within the state and the cultural characteristics of its people and their communities reflect that equilibrium: to the east, extensive sections of remote deserts and mountains where people are scarce; to the west, just beyond the Cascade Range, valleys brimming with people. And the inhabitants of this middle ground boldly declare their regional autonomy: "This isn't Eastern Oregon; we're Central Oregonians!"

Within this long, north-south strip through the center of the state, the Bend area in the mid-section is the most developed and populated. The dry, sunny climate, dramatic mountain views, abundant rivers, streams and lakes, and close-at-hand wilderness and skiing opportunities have attracted many new residents. Big city refugees from Western Oregon, California, and other populous areas, eager to trade smog and traffic jams for a small, progressive ski-resort town, relocated to Bend during a 1970s boom that slowed to a steadier growth in the 1980s. Additionally, the area's proximity to Willamette Valley population centers allows easy access by vacationers. Resorts, condominium/timeshare communities, and ski and tourist facilities contribute greatly to the region's economic stability.

Although mid-Central Oregon offers many of the amenities and cosmopolitan qualities of Western Oregon, the signs of human habitation diminish rapidly outward from Bend's environs. Many relatively wild areas still refresh the eye and spirit. North- and south-Central Oregon both embrace extensive rural countryside and remote deserts, canyons and mountainous sections. The smaller communities, based on timber and agriculture, resemble those of the far-flung northeastern and southeastern portions of the state.

Like first-time, out-of-state visitors, many native Western Oregonians are strangers to the high, dry side of their own state. Introductions to this country east of the Cascades usually begin in the Bend vicinity, for it is highly publicized. And with good reason. Bend has a mind-boggling array of fascinating locations nearby, many within the town itself or in its "suburbs." Indeed, tourism brochures tout the area's scenic and recreational wealth as though Bend were Mother Nature's Disneyland!

This vibrantly busy community of 18,700 people has grown considerably since the first settlers named it "Farewell Bend." At times, the town buzzes with activity as the service hub for more than 75,000 people from the surrounding area, and a stop for traveling recreationists. Bend seems bigger than it really is. As one visitor remarked, "This is the biggest little city I've ever been in!"

A stroll through Bend's downtown reveals why this site first drew camping Indians for generations and, later, white pioneers. The cold waters of the Deschutes River flow directly through town. Huge ponderosa pines line the shore. Eye-catching views of the shining, snow-capped Cascade peaks form a background. Abutting interesting shops and restaurants, the broad, green lawns of Drake Park overlook serene, river-dammed Mirror Pond. Particularly unique in a downtown area, Drake Park is a designated wildlife refuge for large flocks of ducks, Canada geese and swans, along with the occasional gray squirrel, mink, river otter, osprey and bald eagle.

A winding road to the top of Pilot Butte on the eastern side of town provides an excellent vantage point. This reddish volcanic cinder cone rises 500 feet above the surrounding city neighborhoods and affords a 360-degree view of nearly all of the upper Deschutes River Val-

Above: *Canada geese swim the waters around the Brooks-Scanlon Lumber Mill in Bend.* D.C. LOWE
Left: *Wheat.* BRYAN PETERSON

43

Something of a melting pot, Bend draws a broad mixture of residents, ranging from lawyers and doctors through mill workers and artists to the independently wealthy. The contrasts are intriguing. A cowboy and his dog in a battered old pickup truck frequently wait at a stop light beside a three-piece-suited businessman in a Mercedes Benz. Some newcomers, who missed the cultural offerings of their former metropolitan homes, joined forces with long-time residents to create a satisfying variety of local, high-quality concerts, plays and art showings.

Despite its newer, upscale urbanity, complete with computer-related businesses, high-tech industries and research-and-development corporations, Bend still maintains its roots in the timber industry. Along the river, near the middle of town, banners of smoke float above the large DAW Corporation Lumber Mill. These white plumes have reminded local residents of their "mill town" history since 1916, when two mills occupied opposite sides of the river: the Shevlin-Hixon Company mill and the Brooks-Scanlon Company mill.

Not everyone favors these accelerated changes. Many long-time residents remember quieter, simpler times and complain that "big city transplants" have brought with them the same hectic pace and desire for rapid development that they sought to escape. Certainly, not all is perfect in this seemingly idyllic setting. A typical, garish business strip of signs, car dealers, fast-food drive-ins and motels stretches along the edge of town; rush-hour traffic congests the area's outgrown street systems; grumblings and debates about property tax rates and wage levels erupt now and then; and school funding spawns heated discussion. Newcomers find that lucrative employment can be elusive, and low-paying "make-do" jobs can test their initial survival. Locals joke that Bend has the best-educated garbage collectors and service station attendants in the state.

Despite such tarnishes, most Bendites enjoy skiing Mt. Bachelor, flyfishing famed local streams or listening to classical music performed in Drake Park at the annual Cascade Festival of Music, rewards that far outweigh any negatives.

Bend offers an excellent jumping-off point to explore Central Oregon's many natural features and interesting communities. A good place to begin is six miles south of town at the High Desert Museum, a small but ambitious natural history and cultural museum that has big plans. Ever-expanding, high-quality exhibits interpret the arid terrains of the Northwest. Not a typical collection of "look

ley. On a clear day, nine Cascade peaks are visible from its summit. Another promontory with panoramic views of the Cascades is the park-like campus of Central Oregon Community College on Awbry Butte at the western edge of Bend.

Because of Bend's outdoorsy, natural qualities and its proximity to a multitude of recreational opportunities, the city attracts many athletic enthusiasts, including the U.S. Olympic Ski Team, which sometimes trains at the nearby Mt. Bachelor Ski Development. Joggers, bicyclists, hikers, backpackers, downhill and cross-country skiers, rock-climbers, river-runners, kayakers and windsurfers abound. This health-minded segment of the population supports a noticeably large selection of health food stores, exercise spas, ski shops, sporting goods outlets and annual athletic events. The yearly Pole-Peddle-Paddle Race from Mt. Bachelor to Drake Park has become a popular, world-class event.

but do not touch" exhibits, the High Desert Museum emphasizes direct experience. Through a combination of live native animals in amazingly realistic indoor and outdoor habitats, colorful graphics, historical and cultural exhibits, slide and video shows and live presentations, visitors enjoy a telescoped experience of an entire region.

Just beyond the High Desert Museum, Highway 97 enters a tortured landscape of volcanic lava formations. Icy caves, huge cinder cones, imprints of long-vanished trees and extensive lava fields are all accessible by U.S. Forest Service viewing trails and interpretive exhibits.

Fifteen miles south of Bend lies Sunriver, a large, planned development built in 1968 on the former site of a World War II military base, Camp Abbot. The pine-forest-surrounded village, designed to complement its woodsy, natural environment, blends disparate elements. A residential community with shopping mall, fire department, church, private preparatory school, airstrip and forested residential neighborhoods, Sunriver also is a resort centered around a large, elegant lodge, complete with golf courses, swimming pools, tennis courts, bike paths and canoeing. Sunriver's location along a huge meadow threaded by the winding Deschutes River, with the green Cascade Mountains on the near horizon. The community even boasts its own excellent nature center offering exhibits, classes and field trips.

South of Sunriver, nearly 100 miles of deep timber country represents one of the world's most extensive stands of ponderosa pine, interrupted only occasionally by a grassy meadow. Human settlements, few and far between, consist of small forest towns like La Pine, Gilchrist, Crescent, Chemult and Chiloqrin.

To the east of Bend, beyond irrigated croplands, ranches and juniper woods, rises the long, north-south hump of Horse Ridge. Highway 20 crosses this rise along the upper edge of a deep, bone-dry canyon where a prehistoric river flowed. At the head of this canyon, hauntingly beautiful lava beds, sandy hollows, twisted juniper trees and Indian pictographs invite hikers to explore quiet retreats. This is the Badlands, a study area being considered for wilderness designation. Beyond Horse Ridge, the highway sets its course across the Millican Valley and more than 100 miles of High Desert between Bend and Burns. Just southeast of the little one-store wayside of Millican, Pine Mountain rises from the wide plain, its open summit giving seemingly limitless views southeastward into the Northern Great Basin Desert. Taking advantage of the clear, dry, 6,395-foot-elevation air, Pine

Mountain Observatory, operated by the University of Oregon, houses one of the Pacific Northwest's largest telescopes.

To the north of Horse Ridge, approximately 40 miles, nestled in a green valley below rimrock-topped slopes, the town of Prineville in the Crooked River area clings to its reputation as the "West's last frontier." A strong Old West flavor—cowboy hats, boots and Levis—permeates the streets. Situated at the edge of the pine-clad Ochoco Mountains, Prineville is also a mill town. Loggers in tin hard-hats and brightly-colored suspenders mingle with the cowboys. Not surprisingly, the town hosts both the Central Oregon Timber Festival and the well known Crooked River Round-up rodeo.

A 21-mile drive northwest of Bend on Highway 20 leads across dry, open stands of juniper mixed with sagebrush flats and ranchlands. Looming ever closer, the high, snow-covered Cascade peaks attract photographers along this scenic road, earnestly aiming their lenses to-

Above: *The High Desert Museum in Bend displays fascinating recreations of pioneer life.* DIANE ENSIGN
Facing page, top: *Mt. Bachelor towers above Todd Lake in the Three Sisters Wilderness.* LARRY GEDDIS
Bottom: *Skiers familiar with Central Oregon's winter charms line up at Mt. Bachelor's ski lift.* CINDY McINTYRE

ward the western skyline. At the very foot of the mountains, at the edge of the ponderosa pine forest, the colorful little town of Sisters evokes thoughts of a western movie set. The entire business district has adopted an Old West architectural motif and successfully salvaged a sagging economy through tourism. The source of the town's name is plainly evident at its western edge, where stunning views of the tri-peaks of the Three Sisters Mountains tower above broad, green meadows. These snowy summits, known in pioneer times as Faith, Hope and Charity, serve as the mega-landmarks of mid-Central Oregon. In the pastures below this landscape, llamas graze on the well known Patterson Ranch. Llamas are fast becoming almost as common in Central Oregon as cattle, and the area has become known as the llama-breeding capital of the U.S.

As Highway 20 continues northwest of Sisters, it passes through magnificent stands of large ponderosa pines with their jig-saw patterns of cinnamon-red bark. Just beyond Black Butte Ranch, a former cattle operation converted into one of Oregon's finest resorts, a paved side road turns off to the north at the base of cone-shaped Black Butte. This leads five miles through the pines to the isolated mountain village of Camp Sherman, in a spectacular setting of green meadows below the snowy mountains. The crystal-clear Metolius River, a famed flyfishing stream, bubbles forth from nearby icy cold springs. Camp Sherman's name hails from a time around the turn of the century when Sherman County farmers from the open wheat country to the northeast traveled here to camp and refresh themselves after the hot, dusty summer harvests.

Above: Morning sunlight bathes the Crooked River and Smith Rock. SCOTT PRICE
Right: If cattle represent the Old West, llamas well may represent the New West: many Central Oregon ranchers now breed the popular animals for profit. LEONARD NOLT

The wide Deschutes River Valley to the north of Bend unfolds a semi-arid, rugged land of rimrocks, sagebrush flats, irrigated ranches and farmlands, and some of the world's most extensive juniper forests. The Deschutes' waters make the Redmond-Madras area the agricultural center of the valley, where grow crops of alfalfa, rye, oats, wheat, barley, peppermint, potatoes, grass and hay. Dairy and beef cattle, as well as llamas, also grace these plateau farmlands.

Between Redmond and Madras, where the Metolius River from the west and the Crooked River from the east converge with the Deschutes, a narrow, deep gorge known as the Cove Palisades is located at the backwaters of Lake Billy Chinook, created by Round Butte Dam. Downstream another reservoir, Lake Simtustus, backs up behind Felton Dam. These long, canyon-enclosed lakes provide popular areas for fishing and water skiing, and there is an excellent campground at Cove Palisades.

On the Crooked River upstream from the Cove a few miles, the startling spires of Smith Rocks State Park come into view. These immense, reddish-tan formations, with the river winding directly below in a sharp bend around the rocks, offer colorfully dramatic views for picnickers, hikers and photographers. They have become world-famous among rock-climbers, and scores of brightly-clothed people commonly clamber and dangle by ropes on the cliffs. With increased used, accidents, unfortunately, also have become more frequent, a few of them fatal.

Below Lake Simtustus, the Deschutes Canyon takes on a wild, remote quality. For the remainder of its journey northward to join the Columbia River, the lower Deschutes is designated a State Scenic Waterway. Nearly half of this stretch borders the Warm Springs Indian Reservation on the west. After initially losing most of their traditional tribal lands in an 1855 treaty with the U.S. government, the Warm Springs Confederated Tribes transformed loss into success. Because of the rich natural resources of the 640,000 acres they now possess, theirs is one of the most self-sufficient reservations in the U.S. More than 130 years later, the Warm Springs Reservation now boasts a lumber mill; plywood plant; large, modern administration center; a multi-million-dollar resort lodge called Kah-Nee-Ta, with a hot-springs–warmed swimming pool; convention facility, golf course, tennis courts and a new cultural museum. Despite these modern touches, Indians still fish for salmon with nets from traditional wood platforms on the river and capture wild horses locally for use each year at an all-Indian rodeo at nearby Tygh Valley.

River-runners use this untamed portion of the Deschutes and several commercial-guide enterprises offer float trips and white-water thrills.

North-Central Oregon's appearance changes rapidly as the elevation diminishes from 3,623 feet at Bend to around 100 feet where the Deschutes empties into the Columbia. Above the canyon, oak groves begin to appear on the rounded, grassy hills below 11,235' Mt. Hood. Here, the terrain somewhat resembles that of Western Oregon's valleys.

At the northern border of Central Oregon, the historic town of The Dalles was the end of the Oregon Trail for pioneers, who boarded rafts here to float down the hair-

Lake Billy Chinook, almost hidden in its deep canyon, provides a dramatic contrast to distant Mt. Hood soaring into the sky. STEVE TERRILL

raising rapids of the Columbia River Gorge into the Willamette Valley.

The Lewis and Clark expedition had camped here in 1805, on their exploratory journey across the continent. Today, The Dalles is an agricultural trade center for North Central Oregon's famous apple and cherry orchards and wheat crops. Just to the west of The Dalles is the entrance to the Columbia River Gorge National Scenic Area. The picturesque old highway between Rowena and Mosier winds along cliffs and past a nature preserve for rare species of wildflower native to this area. This section of the gorge also bears distinction as one of the finest windsurfing sites in the world, due to the wind-tunnel effect of the canyon.

The fearsome rapids of the gorge that faced the pioneers now have been tamed by a series of dams and navigation locks, transforming the river into a series of placid reservoirs. The Dalles Dam's waters now cover Celilo Falls,

Western Juniper

The tree without a shape of its own

Right: *Some of the most extensive western juniper forests in the world shade the Redmond-Bend area.* JANIS MIGLAVS
Far right: *Eastern Oregon's junipers grow as high as 50 feet and as thick as 18 feet.*
GAIL DENHAM

Not only do the gnarled shapes of juniper trees add a distinctive, scenic touch to the drylands of Eastern Oregon, they also contribute a fragrance. After a summer thunderstorm, the strong, aromatic combination of sagebrush and juniper is particularly pungent. To anyone who has spent considerable time in the arid regions of Oregon, this smell triggers pleasant memories of hikes in open vistas and favorite camping places.

Another distinctive quality about the western juniper is its lack of any particularly distinctive shape. A walk through a grove of these trees quickly demonstrates that no two are quite alike. They are impersonators, taking on the forms of oaks, maples, pines, cedars, manicured ornamental shrubs and even cultured Japanese bonzai trees.

The scratchy, gray-green foliage, thin, shredded bark, and blue, hard berries make this evergreen easy to identify. The "berries" are actually tiny cones that do not open like other conifer cones. Native American Indians used the juniper berry as an herb for cooking and medicinal purposes.

The western juniper is the most arid-adapted tree native to Oregon. On dry, rocky ridges it may appear as a twisted, large shrub, while in other areas with more moisture, it may grow to heights of 50 feet or more. Oregon's largest known juniper, located in the Lost Forest of northern Lake County, towers 70 feet high with a trunk diameter of 18 feet. Some of the most extensive western juniper forests in the world shade mid-Central Oregon in the Bend-Redmond-Madras-Prineville areas.

Counted among the oldest growing Oregon trees, even the dead, weathered snags of junipers survive for decades. The wood of these trees, extremely hard and durable, inspires a joke common among High Desert ranchers, that a juniper fence post will wear out two sets of post holes.

where untold generations of Indians once fished. Upstream 24 miles, past the mouth of the Deschutes River, is the John Day Dam, which generates more power than any other single dam in the world.

About two miles up the Columbia from the John Day Dam is the mouth of the river for which this dam is named. The lower John Day River, a State Scenic Waterway, winds through some of Oregon's most extensive wheat-growing country in the open, rolling Columbia Plateau. Only a few small, widely-separated communities like Wasco, Moro, Grass Valley and Condon interrupt seas of wheat, flowing like green ocean waves in the spring breezes or standing silently golden in the still, hot days of summer.

Some isolated villages such as Shaniko, the former world-class wool shipping station, now are largely deserted ghost-town shadows of former boom-times. Antelope, once a bustling frontier stage stop, recently received national news attention when it successfully resisted "annexation" into a wealthy Indian guru's nearby commune, Rajneeshpuram. The power struggle for civic control of Antelope ended when the commune's own internal strife caused it to self-destruct. Now that the guru and his followers are gone, Antelope is again peaceful and quiet, just the way the locals seem to prefer it.

Not far to the east of Antelope, the elevation drops to the canyon country of the John Day River. The name of the main town of this remote area, Fossil, reflects the geological history of its surroundings. The open, semi-arid hills of this district display multi-colored strata of volcanic ash formations that bear fossils of prehistoric animals and plants as old as 40 million years. The John Day Fossil Beds National Monument separated into three sections along the river, with two of these units located on the lower stretch of the John Day. The Painted Hills unit contains the most brightly colored "badlands" formations within the monument. Intense bands of reds, yellows, greens and buffs give a rainbow appearance to the barren, rounded hills. During particularly moist springtimes, masses of wildflowers add to the display and attract many photographers. The Clarno unit offers a picnic area with interpretive displays and a self-guided trail tour to a large, eroded formation known as the Palisades.

Nearby, along Pine Creek, the Hancock Field Station, operated by the Oregon Museum of Science and Industry in Portland, serves as a science camp for youngsters. The rustic facility was founded in 1953 under the expert

The mighty Columbia River east of Rowena Crest still funnels travelers, attracts settlers and supports industries, just as it did during the last century. D.C. LOWE

guidance of Lon Hancock, a Portland amateur paleontologist who made many important discoveries in the Clarno Formation. Specializing in the teaching of paleontology and other natural science subjects, "Camp Hancock" has launched many beginning students upon successful careers as scientists and naturalists.

South-Central Oregon retains a character distinctly its own. Named for the Indians of the district, this Klamath Basin country is a land of open sagebrush, pine, juniper, lakes, marshes and rivers. Situated within this big basin is the second-largest city east of the Cascades, Klamath Falls, with a population of 17,100. The town overlooks the southern end of gigantic Upper Klamath Lake, where it empties into smaller Lake Ewana by the connecting, mile-long Link River. A small dam now blocks the large lake's outlet where the city's namesake falls once were located. Two green parks grace the shores of these lakes. The Favell Museum of Western Art and Indian Artifacts draws visitors to the downtown area, where many of the community's homes, businesses and public service

buildings are heated by geothermal energy. The city straddles an underground pressure cooker of hot water and steam thought to be one of the largest geothermal areas in the world. This low-cost source of heat even warms the city streets, melting winter snow and ice.

Klamath Falls exudes a strong Old West, outdoors atmosphere. Fishing and hunting stories are overheard on the streets. The Native American influence is strongly felt here, and an annual "Pow Wow Days" celebration features an Indian rodeo, parade and traditional tribal dances. Agricultural crops and cattle ranching lead the Klamath Basin's economy. To the southeast of Klamath Falls irrigated flats along the Lost River grow cold-resistant strains of oats, barley and potatoes. Timber resources also long have been an important part of the economic picture, and Collier State Park, near Chiliquin at the north end of Upper Klamath, offers a museum that displays one of the largest collections of logging equipment in the U.S.

The Upper Klamath National Wildlife Refuge and other refuges attract major flocks of migratory birds along the Pacific Flyway. Hundreds of bald eagles winter in the Klamath Basin, ranking it among North America's largest concentrations of this regal national symbol. Birders thrill to the spectacle of countless birds against sunsets reflected in the lake and its marshes, the alpine silhouette of Mt. McLaughlin looming on the skyline.

To the east of the Klamath Basin, the timbered heights of Fremont National Forest contain the little-visited, rocky crags of the Gearhart Mountain Wilderness. A bit farther to the northeast, the summit of Winter Ridge offered explorer John C. Frémont his first view of the northern portion of the immense Great Basin Desert. Here, tree growth abruptly ends and the expansive, sagebrush-covered basin-and-range country of Southeastern Oregon begins.

Highway 31, along the edge of the pine forest, traces the northwestern rim of this massive interior bowl of aridity. This is classic cattle country: sagebrush flats hemmed in by rimrocks in the distance. A few miles north of the little town of Silver Lake, sandy Fort Rock Valley exposes the dry bed of a Pleistocene lake. Jutting from the middle of the brushy plain, the immense, starkly dramatic walls of Fort Rock can be seen from miles away in the desert. The reddish-tan, sheer-faced walls of the rock tower more than 300 feet high, and stretch more than a third of a mile along this natural amphitheater. Although the "fort" originally formed as a volcanic tuff ring crater with

sloping sides, the eroding wave action of prehistoric Fort Rock Lake gradually created its vertical walls. The south side was completely washed away, creating a wide entrance into the huge, bowl-like interior.

Fort Rock inspires a powerfully awesome feel of the ancient transformations of the earth: of changing climates, dying ice age lakes and the struggles of vanished prehistoric people. Approximately one mile to the west, a rocky promontory contains Cow Cave (usually called Fort Rock Cave) where 13,500-year-old artifacts of the early inhabitants of this valley have been excavated.

This is a harsh, boldly broken, volcanic land. Presiding above it, on the northwestern skyline, is the nearly-8,000-foot presence of Newberry Crater in the forested Paulina Mountains. This immense crater contains Paulina and East lakes, along with campgrounds, two backwoods resorts and one of the world's largest flows of

Above: Not surprisingly, this stone stockade" in the High Desert of Lake County has earned the name Fort Rock. ALAN D. ST. JOHN
Left: Oregon Museum of Science and Industry's field station, "Camp Hancock," draws aspiring natural scientists to the rich hills near Clarno, Wheeler County. ALAN D. ST. JOHN
Above left: John Day Formation-Miocene ash sediments, in Blue Basin, typify John Day Fossil Beds National Monument. DAVID JENSEN
Facing page: Shaniko still echoes with bootsteps on boardwalks. LEONARD NOLT

51

Above: *Klamath Falls' annual Pow Wow Days celebration introduces many visitors to traditional Indian dancing.* J & E BARBOUR
Center: *A traditional Indian fisherman nets autumn Chinook salmon at Shearars Falls on the Deschutes River.* CHRIS LUNESKI
Right: *Weatherbeaten trees, Black Crater, in the Three Sisters Wilderness.* D.C. LOWE
Facing page: *The Palisades, Clarno Unit of John Day Fossil Beds National Monument.* BILL STORMONT

volcanic obsidian glass. Scattered about the Fort Rock area, an abundance of other interesting natural features resulted from vulcanism: Hole-in-the-Ground, a mile-wide depression created by an enormous underground explosion; the Devil's Playground, a large contorted area of lava beds; and a 70-foot-deep earthquake fissure called Crack-in-the-Ground.

Such are the varied faces of this volcanic land, Central Oregon. Its beauty and accessibility attract visitors and residents alike. Population experts predict that by the year 2000, the rapidly developing mid-state, tri-county area will grow from slightly fewer than 85,000 people to more than 135,000. How best to preserve the region's pleasant natural attributes and lifestyle, while still

wisely managing economic development, challenges Central Oregon's future. Increasing clashes between environmental groups and the timber, cattle and hydroelectric industries highlight inevitable differences of opinion. But only carefully weighed compromises and new, creative solutions will maintain a healthy balance over time. The undauntable, pioneering spirit of Central Oregon will, no doubt, find solutions to its growing pains, as it has in the past.

Lava Lands

Right: *Lava Butte, a typical volcanic cinder cone, rises 500 feet above Highway 97 and Deschutes County.* WALT ANDERSON
Facing page: *Sunrise on Newberry Crater looking north to other Cascade peaks, Deschutes National Forest.* GEORGE WUERTHNER

Central Oregon is a young, volatile and volcanic landscape. South of Bend are some of the geologically youngest lava flows within the continental United States (other than at Mt. St. Helens).

The most noticeable formation, Lava Butte, rises 500 feet above nearby Highway 97. This open, reddish-colored promontory is a typical cinder cone located along a fissure that channeled molten lava to the surface. A road winds to the top of this butte and a seasonally-manned Forest Service fire lookout tower and interpretive display. A viewing trail follows the rim of the 180-foot-deep crater and provides amazing vistas of the surrounding country, including the snowy peaks of the Cascade Range to the west.

Spreading immediately below, are approximately 10 square miles of beds of dark, twisted lava that flowed forth from Lava Butte when it erupted nearly 6,200 years ago. A Forest Service-operated visitor center located at the base of the butte includes high-quality exhibits that explain in detail the volcanic surroundings. This excellent center also provides staff and volunteer naturalists to answer questions, and educational brochures and books with self-guided nature trails that lead into the adjoining lava beds.

On the east side of Highway 97 and one mile south of the visitor center is Lava River Cave. This 1.2-mile-long lava tube features stairs that provide easy access to a brochure-guided trail exploring the cave's entire length. Lava River cave is one of the longest uncollapsed lava tubes in the Pacific Northwest.

Rising to nearly 8,000 feet to the southeast, the forested heights of Newberry Volcano form the volcanic focal point of the area. The varying peaks of this collapsed shield volcano, also called the Paulina Mountains, rise above slopes scattered with many interesting vulcanistic features.

Nearly 400 parasitic cinder cones on the volcano's flanks give the mountain a bumpy, uneven appearance. During a period dating back approximately 6,000 years, several lava flows spilled down the mountainside, engulfing and burning forests in their paths. One such flow on the north slope enveloped trees and slowly cooled and hardened around them. The charred wood eventually rotted away, leaving casts of the vanished trees. This is the Lava Cast Forest, accessible by a 10-mile-long gravel road that turns to the east off Highway 97 by the Sunriver exit. A self-guided, mile-long interpretive trail loops through the area and gives visitors a glimpse into a fiery past period.

Topping the mountain, a spectacular, five-mile-wide caldera, Newberry Crater, cradles two large, blue lakes, East Lake and Paulina Lake. Along a slope between the lakes stretches one of the largest and most recent obsidian glass flows in the world, being less than 2,000 years old. Besides two rustic mountain resorts, several National Forest Campgrounds that provide an opportunity to sleep inside a volcano in the heart of Central Oregon's Lava Lands.

PART III

Southeastern Oregon

Sagebrush, Jackrabbits, Cowboys & Unfettered Vistas

Above: In Malheur County. STEVE TERRILL *Right: In many ways, Southeastern Oregon has changed little in a century.* TIM THOMPSON *Facing page, top: Moonrise over the High Desert near Rome, along the Owyhee River, rivals any scenery in the world* ALAN D. ST. JOHN *Bottom: Owyhee River Reservoir.* DAVID JENSEN *Right: Rugged Owyhee Canyon.* TIM THOMPSON

From Covered Wagons to Horseless Carriages

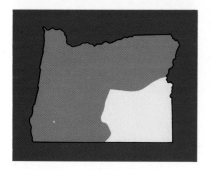

A rainbow promises treasure, and Steens Mountain certainly delivers.
STEVE TERRILL

The reason I've been able to produce some fast horses, is that where I graze them, they have to feed at thirty miles an hour to get enough to eat.

Reub Long, *The Oregon Desert*

The High Desert country of Oregon can be a difficult region for raising horses and cattle, and for other agricultural enterprises, as this humorous anecdote attests. Reub Long, well known philosopher of the desert, spent his entire life ranching these sparse drylands and observed many poorly prepared, would-be homesteaders come and go.

However, others managed to survive upon this arid land, and a few ranches have been operated by the same families for several generations. The long-time resident of Southeastern Oregon generally tolerates no nonsense and knows one must meet nature on its own terms here; but when asked about the country he resides in, he often waxes eloquent with deep convictions about this expansive, sagebrush-covered land that he loves. Human beings do not dominate Southeastern Oregon. The big land and the still-larger sky overwhelm human efforts completely, while the profound stillness is a blank sheet upon which the desert winds write their background music.

The first people to inhabit this far corner of Oregon successfully became masters of desert survival. These prehistoric aboriginal groups moved into the area from the north at the close of the ice age. Although extremely little is known about these early primitive hunter-gatherers, their lifestyle probably resembled that of their descendants, the Northern Paiute Indians.

Large bands of Paiutes were uncommon in Southeastern Oregon, their social structure emphasizing small, widely separated family groups. The meager offerings of the arid Great Basin generally could not provide sufficient food, firewood and other supplies to support large tribes. Some archaeological investigations indicate that there may have been only one Paiute family group for every 100 square miles before the coming of white settlers. Their lifestyle was simple, nomadic and unencumbered. Food consisted of nearly anything edible: roots, shoots, berries, seeds, birds and their eggs, lizards, snakes, fish, insects, rabbits, marmots and other squirrels, mule deer, pronghorn antelope and bighorn sheep all were relished when available. The Paiute groups of the Harney Basin apparently hunted buffalo, too, as early white explorers found skulls and other bones of these huge animals around Malheur and Harney lakes. Why buffalo disappeared here remains unknown.

Winter, a time of scarcity, demanded supplies of dried foods accumulated through the warm months. Starvation probably was all too frequent in severe, extended winters. Paiute camps were Spartan, basically unadorned compared with the artfully elegant tipi assemblages of the larger tribes of Plains Indians to the east. Paiutes constructed temporary, lean-to shelters of local plant materials on the spot, and they sometimes inhabited caves. Mats, usually woven from cattail leaves, formed bed pads or, propped up by short pole frames, chairs to recline against. Various sizes of woven baskets served for gathering, storing and cooking foods, even as

Southeastern Oregon's first human inhabitants carved petroglyphs like this one, on the south slope of Red Butte in the Owyhee River Canyon.
ALAN D. ST. JOHN

women's hats. The indispensable, all-purpose rabbit-skin blanket doubled as bed covering and warm clothing. Twisted sagebrush bark fiber made tough sandals. The Paiutes netted, snared or killed small animals with a dead-fall trap. Primitive bows and stone-point–tipped arrows augmented these hunting methods.

Such was the simple, austere lifestyle of these early Oregonians. Where a modern-day person, wearing adequate clothing and boots and possessing a jackknife, might die within a few days of dehydration and exposure to heat or cold, these skilled desert dwellers survived generation after generation for thousands of years. And they did so mostly naked, wearing sandals and using only the most primitive tools and shelters, through blazingly hot summers and snowy, sub-zero winters.

However, this millennia-old aboriginal society surrendered within less than a century to the arriving white men, whose coming heralded the eclipse of an ancient way of life that could be traced back across a vanished land bridge to Asian roots.

Three Frenchmen—La Valle, Charbonneau and Nadeau—may have been the first whites to see Southeastern Oregon. Embarking upon an incredible adventure across an unmapped, wild continent without sup-

59

plies or guns in 1750, they left a ship on the southern California coast, at the present site of San Diego, and attempted to walk to Quebec in eastern Canada! Whatever prompted this hopeless trek, history does not say. Two of them survived long enough to arrive in what is now Idaho, where they abandoned their fiasco and lived with the local Indians.

In 1818, Donald McKenzie, while investigating the Snake River drainage for the Northwest Fur Company, reached the head of a river in what is now southern Idaho. He sent three Hawaiian members of his crew down this unknown watercourse that flowed toward the west and the present-day Oregon boundary. These south-sea islanders never came back from the wild canyon and it was named in their honor, using the native pronunciation for their islands, "Owyhee."

The first documented exploration of interior Southeastern Oregon was in 1825-1826, when Peter Skene Ogden led about 100 members of a Hudson's Bay Company brigade into the Snake River area to trap for beaver. Six of his men followed a tributary river into the Harney Basin. When Indians wounded and killed several members of the party and stole their furs, these French trappers named the river Malheur, meaning "bad times." Later, the large lake of that area assumed the same name. In the fall of 1826, Ogden himself explored the Harney district, the first of several such trips that continued through 1829. The next white explorer to enter this arid region, in 1831, was another Hudson's Bay employee, John Work. He investigated as far south as the eastern side of Steens Mountain, calling it "Snow Mountain."

In the winter of 1843, that far-ranging pathfinder, Lt. John C. Frémont, with his scout, Kit Carson, led a government survey party through Central Oregon and southeastward, exploring and naming Summer and Abert lakes. The group then progressed south into California and crossed the Sierras.

That same year of 1843 saw huge migrations of settlers coming west on the Oregon Trail begin. This famous trail crossed the Snake River into Oregon near the present sites of Nyssa and Ontario, progressed northwesterly over the Blue Mountains, and down the Columbia River to The Dalles.

In 1845, the Blue Bucket Train was the first to attempt a southerly short-cut through the middle of the High Desert. It was not the last to suffer hardship on this route. Indians attacked one small group of emigrants, composed mainly of the family of Thomas Clark, in Idaho near the Snake River, in 1851. Clark's 19-year-old sister, Grace, was wounded by a gunshot and partly scalped; his mother and younger brother were killed. The survivors endured a miserable trip across the Oregon desert, eventually camping by the Deschutes River at the present site of Bend, where they rested for several days while the injured girl regained her strength.

The military showed interest in Southeastern Oregon by 1859, starting to survey a route for a new road through the region to Salt Lake City. They encountered resistance. In 1860, Captain A. Smith was attacked by Indians. Major Enoch Steen, who was also surveying in the area, brought his cavalry troops to the rescue in the proverbial "nick-of-time," and Steens Mountain today bears his name.

In 1861, the traffic of white travelers through Southeastern Oregon accelerated when gold was discovered in the Blue Mountains to the north. More strikes soon followed in that general area, in Idaho, and in 1862 in the Mormon Basin near the Snake River, north of present-day Ontario. Excited gold seekers streamed through the area on military roads and small settlements coalesced in the Mormon Basin. A way station began business in 1863 at the Ruby Ranch on a road along Jordan Creek. By the following year, a short distance to the east, John Baxter built a hotel-store combination. At first this settlement was called Baxterville, but the name later changed to Jordan Valley. Trappers built the first permanent residence in the Harney Basin in 1862: a simple sod house, located near the present site of the Malheur National Wildlife Refuge headquarters.

The Paiutes observed this increasing activity with concern. When most U.S. Army troops left Oregon during the Civil War, frequent Indian attacks harassed unprotected settlers and travelers. After the war, troops returned and established a number of military camps in the region to quell unrest. By 1868, Indian resistance to white settlement ceased and, with more peaceful conditions, new communities began.

In 1867, another gold strike in the Mormon Basin caused an influx of miners there and two communities soon sprang up: Eldorado and Amelia City, followed by a third, Malheur City. And the booming gold and silver mining town of Silver City, growing since 1864 in the Owyhee Mountains of southwestern Idaho, now was overflowing with nearly 5,000 people. These hard-working men with big appetites demanded plenty of good-quality beef. Although a few settlers on this wild, young

frontier already were raising cattle, their endeavors utilized only a small fraction of the immense rangelands. Wealthy entrepreneurs from California and elsewhere noted the potential of Southeastern Oregon's unclaimed millions of acres of open bunchgrass plains.

As cattle ranches appeared in the region, more communities served as supply and trade centers. In 1872, a small stone house built on the lower Malheur River catered to wagon trains on the Oregon Trail, and fostered the village of Vale. At the western edge of the region, in 1874, the town of Lakeview was born. Paisley and Summer Lake also emerged during this period.

Sheep ranching played a large role in the settling of Southeastern Oregon, for most miners liked a meal of mutton as well as beef. To supply this market, enterprising sheepherders brought their wooly flocks into the region. These early herders were predominantly of Scotch and Irish origins but, later, many Basques also arrived.

The vicinity of the Jordan Valley was particularly noted as sheep country. Although outright range wars between cattle ranchers and sheep men, like those in Central Oregon, occasionally arose, most of these conflicts involved wandering "tramp sheepmen" (and tramp cattlemen as well) who moved onto ranges used by established ranches. In fact, many large cattle operations also ran sheep.

In 1878, one final Indian uprising occurred. The Paiutes in Southeastern Oregon and the Bannocks of southern

Above: Andrews Saloon in the Alvord Basin once rang with the rowdy voices of miners, shepherds and cattlemen. DAVID JENSEN
Facing page, top: Harney County sleeps beneath a beautiful blanket of snow. BRYAN PETERSON
Bottom: The rusting remains of borax works haunt the Alvord Basin. GEORGE WUERTHNER

62

MY COUNTRY 'TIS OF THEE

HARNEY COUNTY SAGEBRUSH SYMPHONY ORCHESTRA
BURNES ORE.

Idaho had been established on reservations which the U.S. government believed solved the earlier hostilities. However, during the Civil War years, government funds for these reservations had been largely rerouted to the military effort. The Indians, inexperienced as farmers and denied access to their tribal hunting and gathering grounds, were left to starve. When a clerical "error" opened a traditional Bannock camas-gathering area in Idaho for white settlement, these Indians reacted.

Under the leadership of Chief Buffalo Horn, the Bannocks influenced the Paiutes of Oregon to join them in a war against the whites. The combined forces of Buffalo Horn and the Paiutes, under Chief Egan, swept through Southern Idaho and Eastern Oregon, burning homes and way stations, killing settlers, travelers, miners, sheepherders and cattle ranchers. The consolidated efforts of the army, a citizen's volunteer militia and friendly Indians finally ended the uprising. The Paiutes of the Harney Basin area were banished to a reservation in Washington, where many died of illnesses and the government claimed their reservation lands. When a small group of Paiutes eventually returned, only a fraction of their original reservation remained.

Eastern Oregon in the meantime earned a reputation for producing fine horses, one man's enterprise in particular adding to this reputation. Bill Brown, beginning in 1882, operated a large horse ranch on the desert between the present locations of Bend and Burns. Brown, known as the "Horse King," sold millions of dollars worth of livestock over the years, but could not maintain his wealth, being excessively generous and following poor business practices. Reportedly, he wrote checks on whatever happened to be handy, whether it was a piece of newspaper or the back of a food can label.

For many years, cattle and other stock that were to be marketed had to be trailed overland long distances to railheads in northern Nevada or as far as Wyoming and Kansas, beyond the Rocky Mountains. However, by 1884, the railroad reached the Snake River area of Oregon and spawned the community of Ontario. With this rail connection, Southeastern Oregon opened itself to the markets of the outside world and an era drew to a close.

Things changed quickly in the region. A new community near the military base of Fort Harney, called Burns (after Scottish poet Robert Burns), opened a post office in 1884. By 1907, the first "horseless carriage" to drive through the town created quite a stir. Beginning in 1909, the offer of government land to U.S. citizens under the

Revised Homestead Act brought a wave of new settlers to the High Desert. Small communities sprouted almost overnight, even in the most remote sections of this sprawling land. By 1921, most had become ghost towns when starry-eyed farmers discovered that the rainfall was miserably scant and soils produced more dust than green crops. Mining boom towns had long since passed their zeniths when the mines played out in the late 1800s. Towns like Eldorado, Amelia City and Malheur City either died or deteriorated toward ghost-town status.

In 1928, the government funded irrigation canal construction projects in the Ontario vicinity along the Snake River, and another agricultural boom resulted. The additions of dams on the Owyhee, Malheur and other water courses transformed the Snake River Valley into a garden oasis of vegetables, fruits, grains and other crops.

When a connecting highway between Burns and Bend opened in 1929, the modern age truly had arrived in remote Southeastern Oregon. Where weary 19th-century wagon trains struggled westward across the baking High Desert for weeks, a 20th-century automobile can make the 130-mile trip in fewer than three hours.

Above: Because early miners liked mutton as well as beef, sheep ranches quickly were established in Southeastern Oregon, especially the Jordan Valley. L.G. HAMMOND
Facing page, top left: Paisley has been as satisfied with its peaceful existence as with the sign on its Chevrolet dealership. © GARY BRAASCH
Top right: Peter French's celebrated round barn, 60' in diameter, still stands on the Malheur National Wildlife Refuge. STEVE ANTELL
Bottom left: A cockeyed old wagon weathers another summer on the Peter French ranch near Frenchglen. JERRY LONG
Bottom right: A cultural pursuit near Burns: The Harney County Sagebrush Symphony Orchestra (no date given). NEG 52629, OREGON HISTORICAL SOCIETY

Era of the Cattle Barons

In the early 1860s, the vast interior rangelands of Southeastern Oregon escaped white settlement. Only a few bands of Paiute Indians wandered the sagebrush plains. Then, in 1869, John S. Devine came to the Alvord Basin in the extreme southeastern corner of the region. He was the first permanent settler to inhabit this huge desert wilderness and he built Oregon's first cattle empire.

Devine, a Californian only 30 years old at the time, came equipped to immediately start a working ranch. He had the financial backing of a wealthy Sacramento meat company owner, W.B. Todhunter, and arrived in Oregon with 3,000 head of cattle, a herd of horses, six vaquero cowhands, a cook and a wagon full of supplies. Devine fancied himself as an aristocrat in the mold of the old Spanish dons and dressed and acted the part.

After claiming the lands of an abandoned military camp, where he established his famed Whitehorse Ranch, Devine greatly expanded his holdings. His stock grazed across the largest part of the country below the east face of Steens Mountain and he added a second operation, the Alvord Ranch. Despite the isolation of his spread, 200 miles from the nearest settlers, Devine used his wealth to create an oasis of refinement. He rode a beautiful white stallion fitted with a silver-adorned saddle, impressed guests with his stable of top-rate racehorses and his well stocked game farm, and lavished on them sumptuous meals of fine foods and wines.

However, by the early 1870s, Devine was no longer alone in his remote, private kingdom. A young man of 23, Peter French, started the P Ranch in the Blitzen Valley in 1872. Backed by the rich assets of Dr. Hugh Glenn, an influential land-owner in the Sacramento Valley and the largest wheat grower in the nation, French also came to the region completely outfitted for ranching.

Eventually, the P Ranch engulfed most of the grazing lands along the west side of Steens Mountain and spawned several satellite ranches, the largest being at Roaring Springs in the Catlow Valley. Although Pete French became a wealthy, powerful man and a legend in the Old West, his life was less than peaceful and pleasant. He married partner Glenn's daughter, but she refused to live on his remote ranch and their marriage ended in divorce. In the tumultuous years that followed, Glenn was murdered by one of his employees, leaving French with legal problems and debts, and he lost large amounts of his lands. Indians attacked French's ranches and cowhands. More settlers came to the area, involving French in many bitter disputes over boundary claims and water rights. French's terse, uncompromising business methods lost him many friendships and created serious animosities with most neighboring ranchers. Peter French lost his life in 1897 when a neighboring rancher shot him during a heated argument.

Meanwhile, due to forfeiture of illegal land holdings and serious losses of cattle during the severe winters of 1887 to 1890, John Devine filed bankruptcy. Henry Miller, a shrewd and powerful German cattleman from California, bought out Devine but retained him as manager of his Oregon properties and gave him back the deed to the Alvord Ranch and all its livestock. Miller must have admired the proud Devine, allowing the pseudo-nobleman to retain part of his honor and great empire, where he lived the remainder of his life.

After Peter French's violent death, Henry Miller added some of French's former lands to his ever-growing holdings throughout the West, and founded the famous Pacific Land and Livestock Company. When Miller died in 1916, he owned the world's largest cattle empire. A colorful era closed.

The Whitehorse, Alvord and Roaring Springs Ranches still operate, and Pete French's famous round barn, which he used for breaking horses, can be seen near the Malheur Wildlife Refuge.

Above: *Peter French.*
NEG 75236, OREGON HISTORICAL SOCIETY
Right: *Eating dust.*
BRYAN PETERSON
Facing page: *John Devine.*
NEG. 4145, OREGON HISTORICAL SOCIETY

Sagebrush & Elbow Room

Above: *Obsidian on Glass Mountain, Harney County.* WALT ANDERSON
Right: *Snow dusts the slopes of Steens Mountain after a spring storm. The east slope of the mountain is a fault-block escarpment.* GEORGE WUERTHNER
Facing page: *The rustic Frenchglen Hotel in Frenchglen caters to motorists traveling the Steens Mountain Loop.* JANIS MIGLAVS

Of the three regions east of the Cascades in Oregon, the High Desert of the southeastern corner most vividly contrasts to the state's popular image of rainy weather and lush forests.

This relentlessly arid, barren country does not attract retirees to soothing relaxation in green, park-like surroundings. The dramatic environment demands complete attention and stimulates the senses. It is dry, scratchy, prickly and rough. Instead of the gentle, rounded lines of damper, wooded climates, this lean, angular land gives an impression of raw-boned, virile youth. The lack of heavy precipitation has not allowed erosion to smooth the sharp edges of its face. At the same time, cracks and wrinkles, ravines and canyons lend a weathered, scarred appearance to its countenance. This terrain has known rough times and passed through trials of volcanic fire and gut-wrenching, inner turbulence. An inscrutable, wizened quality here speaks simultaneously of both youth and extreme age—a timeless backwash where long-vanished, prehistoric waves deposited seashells onto today's dry, fossilized desert shorelines.

Overhead, a wide sky achieves the deepest shade of clear, dry-air blue. Few clouds obscure the scintillating light, which blinds with its mid-day ferocity on a white alkali flat. The desert is married to the sun. Its shadows mirror the bright orb's arcs across the sky. The slanting rays of morning and evening reveal the contrasting textures of the landscape, while at the solar zenith it becomes a bleached, homogeneous whole.

Why come to the desert? Can its parched, open and distant spaces compare with Oregon's pleasant forests, high alpine meadows, pastoral valley countrysides and ocean beaches? The alien immensity of Southeastern Oregon's vast deserts, awesome fault-block ranges, yawning gorges and bleak lack of trees can be unsettling. The sweeping, wild immensity of it makes a visitor feel small.

Too many people see only the desert's surface, noticing what it is not rather than what it actually is. Because the basic plant growth is low shrubs, the eyes quite naturally focus on the distant horizon. But beyond the mind-set that requires trees and soft, green grass, an awareness of the High Desert's subtle attributes deserves its own focus.

The spectacular geological formations of Southeastern Oregon give the region a rugged beauty unique to the High Desert. One of the best places to gain a broad perspective on the lay of the region's land is from atop Steens Mountain.

Born of tremendous convulsions in the bowels of the earth, this ancient massif shoulders its glaciated bulk 9,733 feet into the clear desert sky. As the highest point in the entire northern Great Basin, Steens Mountain provides incredible views of Southeastern Oregon, large sections of Idaho and Nevada, and even mountains in Washington and California. The arid climate keeps this a barren, unforested range. Other than groves of quaking aspen, only two canyons support small stands of Sierran white fir.

Ascending this rarified, high-altitude world does not require days of strenuous backpacking. A 68.6-mile-long gravel and dirt road, known as the Steens Mountain Loop, winds its way upward to the crest of the mountain, rewarding motorists with one of the most awe-inspiring scenic drives in all the Northwest. A good departure point for this trip is the small community of Frenchglen, located 60 miles south of the city of Burns on Highway 205. In this town named for the famed local cattle baron of the 1800s, Peter French, and his partner, Hugh Glenn, the picturesque era seems to live on. The

Borax hot springs like this one in the Alvord Basin once employed Chinese laborers and 16-mule teams as part of a vigorous borax processing industry. STEPHEN TRIMBLE

passing small meadows and little lakes. Unbelievably, this alpine-like setting is the heart of arid Southeastern Oregon.

In autumn, these groves transform themselves into a brilliant gold and reddish-orange blanket spread over the open slopes. Visitors at that time of year can stroll off into the soothing depths of these aspen groves, pick comfortable spots among the white-barked trunks, and lie back to peer up through the whispering yellow and red foliage against the intense blue of the high-altitude sky. As the wind-blown, golden leaves float down, the hurry-scurry, 20th-century world suddenly seems far away.

Higher still, a turn-off leads to the Kiger Gorge Viewpoint at the very edge of the north-facing rim of one of the world's colossal, textbook-perfect glacial gorges. From here, the land literally drops away at the observer's feet, and the view defies description. The main loop road continues eastward atop the Steens crest to another turn-off that ends at the Wildhorse Lake Viewpoint. Leading from the edge of the viewpoint parking area, a very steep road ascends to a radio repeater station: the highest elevation on Steens Mountain and also the highest point accessible by vehicles in Oregon (four-wheel-drives only, however).

From this lofty vantage point, the seemingly endless views in all directions scan a magnificent, high-altitude realm of bighorn sheep, and these sure-footed animals sometimes appear along the rocky chasms that drop away below the summit. Several rare and endangered flowers and other small plants occur in this fragile, high-elevation ecosystem and visitors should avoid trampling the area. To the south and immediately below a large, glacially-excavated, hanging valley (the geological term is "cirque") contains Wildhorse Lake. Still farther to the south, the broken ridges and humps of the remote Pueblo Mountains give way to the vast Black Rock Desert country of northern Nevada.

Directly below, at the eastern base of Steens Mountain, the huge, dry, north-south trough of the Alvord Basin once held a prehistoric lake. Brushy sand dunes literally drift along the edges of alkali flats in the barren Alvord Desert. From the mountain's distant perspective, the desert resembles a gigantic, white, paved parking lot shimmering in the sun. Situated in the Steens rain-shadow, this Alvord country is the truest desert area within Oregon.

Remnant lakes and streams still persist in this baked basin, some with their own unique, isolated species of fish. The small, shallow lakes are quite alkaline, often

Frenchglen Hotel, an operating business and a state historical wayside, offers eight rental rooms and home-style cooking served at a large communal table.

The Loop Road, generally in fairly good condition, is usually free of snow from mid-July through October. However, rapid and unpredictable weather changes at the higher elevations favor automobiles with adequate clearance and good traction. The route leads east from Frenchglen and, after crossing the Blitzen River, immediately begins its ascent of the long western side of Steens Mountain. This is no cone-shaped peak. More like a huge, rugged ridge, this fault-block range formed some 10 million years ago when a gigantic fracture developed, uplifting it. Thus, while the western slant of the mountain gradually slopes upward, the eastern side drops away in a dizzying, near-vertical precipice. The road first passes through a fragrant juniper forest, but, after climbing still higher, enters an open, grassy plateau where huge, glaciated gorges open to the west. Here, the road wends its way through grove after grove of aspens,

simply *playas* that evaporate in summer. One, Borax Lake, is fed by hot springs that contain large amounts of sodium borate, a substance used in cleaning agents. The crusty, white crystals that form here once supplied a borax industry at the turn of the century. Chinese laborers collected deposits, processed them into purified borax crystals, and sacked and shipped them 130 miles to Winnemucca, Nevada, by 16-mule-team wagon. Two historic and remote cattle ranches, the Whitehorse Ranch and the Alvord Ranch, began here in the late 1800s and still operate.

Only a few small desert outposts such as Fields, Andrews and Denio exist in this big, lonely land. To the east, beyond the wild Trout Creek Mountains, McDermitt straddles the Oregon-Nevada border along Highway 95. For many years, until it closed in 1984, the Whitehorse Saloon here served thirsty buckaroos, tired and dry from their work on the range. This colorful establishment was famous for being half in Nevada and half in Oregon, with a line painted across the middle of the floor to separate the two states. Customers wishing to play the slot machines and gamble merely had to step over the demarcation into the Nevada side of the building.

This little-traveled, interior corner of the Pacific Northwest often is called the "ION Country," because Idaho, Oregon and Nevada all meet here. Through this land east of Steens Mountain and the Alvord Basin flow the waters of the Owyhee River. As it winds through rocky corridors and 1,000-foot sheer-walled gorges, age-old Indian pictographs and petroglyphs silently witness its northward journey to rendezvous with the Snake River.

Much of this inaccessible canyonlands is wilder and more remote than any other officially-designated wilderness area south of the Canadian border. Visited mainly by seasonal river runners, an occasional rockhound or a rancher tending his far-ranging cattle, the Owyhee possesses a mysterious, haunting beauty all its own. Sections of the Owyhee are listed among the state's several scenic waterways. In many respects, its sedimentary sandstone formations resemble the canyon country of Utah. Through eons, the river has eroded and sculpted multicolored "badlands" of picturesque spires and balanced rocks and arches, particularly in the Leslie Gulch vicinity. Near the small, riverside community of Rome, the "Rome Ruins" formations resemble ancient Roman architecture and give the settlement its name.

Except where Highway 95 crosses the river at Rome, just a few, rough, unmarked jeep trails penetrate the interior

Majestic "Rome Ruins" formations shadow the Owyhee River near Rome. ALAN D. ST. JOHN

Owyhee drainage and only motorists outfitted with good maps, extra gas and water, and four-wheel-drive vehicles should venture into this rugged back country. A passing thunderstorm can quickly turn these dirt tracks to sticky gumbo mud, while resulting flash-floods can obliterate a trail where it crosses a formerly dry wash. A hopelessly mired auto could mean a 50- to 75-mile walk out from some locations. Therefore, self-reliance is the key to safe exploration and camping here. Access by boat is possible along Lake Owyhee, where the lower river has been impounded behind the Owyhee Dam. A shady, grassy state park located near the dam and a small resort offer boat rentals, food and overnight accommodations. Fishing enthusiasts tout the little-known Owyhee for its generous catches of bass, crappie, catfish and trout. During spring, when the water is high, guided wilderness river-running trips put in at Rome and end at the reservoir.

Like most of Eastern Oregon, the Owyhee country exhibits many volcanic features, such as hot springs and ex-

Horned Lizards

Miniature Monsters of the Desert Sand

Right: *Short-horned lizard.*
Far right: *Desert horned lizard.*
ALAN D. ST. JOHN PHOTOS

The bizarre, spiny appearance and odd body shape of the well known "horny toad," or horned lizard, cause them to resemble tiny dinosaurs or dragons. Of the two species native to Oregon, the desert horned lizard sports large, crown-like spines at the back of the head and a scattering of smaller spines on the body, legs and tail. Adults are usually three to five inches in length. The second variety, the short-horned lizard, shows smaller and fewer spines. It is also not so large as the other species. Sometimes called the pygmy horned lizard, the short-horned lizard has a maximum length of no more than three inches. Both species are basically brown or gray with darker markings, although coloration varies greatly from one area to another as they match their habitats quite well. Desert horned lizards generally exhibit brighter colors, often rusty-orange speckling.

All horned lizards (there are 14 species in North America) have wide, flat bodies and short tails. This low profile allows them to quickly burrow into the sand when seeking escape. The spines discourage hungry predators.

Horned lizards prefer open areas with scattered bushes and soil that is sandy or gravelly. However, both species rarely share the same location. In Oregon, the desert horned lizard inhabits the low, hot, arid basins of the southeastern part of the state. The short-horned lizard, more tolerant of cold, scurries throughout the open sagebrush country of Eastern Oregon, and even ranges to the top of the Cascade Mountains in open lava-dust areas along the crest.

The favored food of all horned lizards is ants, although they feed on other insects and spiders well. Reproduction differs in the two species: the desert horned lizard lays eggs, while the short-horned lizard bears its young alive.

Although popular as pets, these lizards usually do not live long in captivity and are best left in the wild. In fact, the short-horned lizard has been placed on the protected species list in Oregon.

tensive lava beds. In the vicinity of historic Jordan Valley, known for its generations of Basque sheepherders, the Jordan Craters contain some of North America's most recent lava flows. A little-known point of interest is located a few miles west of Jordan Valley: the grave of Jean Baptiste Charbonneau, the son of famed Sacajawea. He was born while his mother was a member of the Lewis and Clark Expedition and she held him in her arms when she first saw the Pacific Ocean in 1805. Charbonneau died of pneumonia in 1866 while staying at the old Ruby Ranch way station once situated at this site.

A pioneer stage road north of Jordan Valley leads to the reddish rock walls of Succor Creek Canyon. The route follows the stream through a colorful, narrow aperture to a state campground. The unusual name for this watercourse has had two different spellings over the years, depending upon the supposed source of the name. One version maintains that pioneers found aid or "succor" there from either thirst or an Indian attack. Another tells of early miners who were played for "suckers." Still another says that the name is simply derived from the fish of that species in the stream. An 1895 stage stop post office in the canyon spelled it "Sucker," perhaps indicating the correct version.

A few miles north of the dam, the Owyhee leaves its canyon and wends its way into green, irrigated fields. This watered oasis, where the Malheur River also enters the Snake River Valley, forms the agricultural hub of Southeastern Oregon. The local centers of commerce include Ontario, Nyssa and Vale. Crops of wheat, alfalfa, mint, corn, sugar beets, onions, potatoes, fruits and other produce thrive here.

The area's population consists of several different ethnic groups. Historically, the area attracted immigrants by virtue of its location along the Oregon Trail. Wagon wheel ruts from this famous route can still be seen south of Vale at a designated interpretive site. Basque sheep ranchers and Dutch immigrants came to the region around the turn of the century and, during World War II, the government established a Japanese internment camp in Cow Hollow. The Japanese were allowed to work in the fields of local farms and, after the war, many stayed in the area and purchased land. Now, Japanese families operate some of the largest, most successful farms here. In more recent years, many farm workers of Mexican origin settled in the valley and integrated themselves into the local communities.

The view to the north of Steens Mountain takes in the entire Harney Basin. Far below, the vast green marshes and open waters of Malheur and Harney lakes, protected by the Malheur National Wildlife Refuge, attract great numbers of waterfowl on their seasonal migrations along the Pacific Flyway. Information and displays at the refuge headquarters at the south edge of Malheur Lake provide sources for understanding the area's complex ecology. Another excellent resource for the study and protection of Southeastern Oregon's ecosystems is the nearby Malheur Field Station, operated by a consortium of Oregon and Washington colleges and universities. It offers field courses in various natural science subjects, and provides dormitory and cafeteria services. Located in ideal outdoor-classroom surroundings, the station takes full advantage of the wildlife refuge, Diamond Craters, Malheur Cave, Steens Mountain and the Alvord Basin to teach the fascinating local natural history.

The Owyhee River breaks intimidated the early travelers and still attract but few hikers. DAVID JENSEN

Above: *Steens Mountain on the horizon overlooks the wildlife-rich Malheur National Wildlife Refuge.*
RON SPOMER
Right: *A botanist studies specimens atop Steens Mountain.*
GEORGE WUERTHNER

A 25-mile drive north to the city of Burns on Highway 205 from the refuge takes travelers across the connecting waters of Malheur and Harney lakes, now the state's largest inland body of water. Just a few years ago these lakes were smaller and separated by dry land, marshes and playas, collectively called the Narrows. The levels of both lakes rose dramatically in recent years, during a period of above-average precipitation, submerging a railroad track, several farms and the original highway. The road now crosses on several miles of a narrow strip of raised roadway bounded on both sides by water.

Burns is the business center for the area's cattle industry and a large wood products company supplied by the timbered Blue Mountains to the north. The days of 19th-century cattle barons gave way to agribusiness in Southeastern Oregon. Smaller, private ranches still exist, but large corporations dominate the scene. Traditional cowboy hats, boots and horse tack share the range now with high-tech accoutrements. Modern ranchers may now spend as much time managing business in front of their computers as they do in the saddle.

To the west of Burns spread more than a hundred miles of open sagebrush rangelands culminating at the slopes of the Cascade Mountains in Central Oregon. This is the former territory of the famous "Horse King," Bill Brown, where wild horses still roam the windswept High Desert. At Glass Buttes, where Paiute Indians gathered volcanic obsidian glass for arrowheads and other implements, remnant chippings dropped by aboriginal flintknappers still can be seen.

Gazing westward through field glasses from Steens Mountain's summit, the eye scans alternating basins and table-like escarpment-edged mountains that extend to the distant horizon the northwestern reaches of North America's immense interior Great Basin, a fearfully arid place that has no drainage to the sea. The few watercourses that flow from the region's higher elevations dissipate rather than grow as gravity pulls them toward extinction in dry alkali playas.

The massive, alternating humps and depressions of this geologically faulted basin-and-range country seem to march endlessly westward. Place names such as Catlow Valley, Lone Mountain, Antelope Butte, Sagehen Butte, Blizzard Gap, Dry Valley, Lonegrave Butte, Coyote Hills and Wildcat Mountain all paint a picture of a landscape of sagebrush and unfettered vistas. The land's enormity dwarfs the scant human population and the few settlements: Wagontire, Plush, Adel, Valley Falls, Paisley,

Summer Lake and Christmas Valley. The largest city in this southwestern section of Oregon's desert corner, Lakeview, musters a population of 2,800. Situated in an open valley, separated from the High Desert country just to the east by a pine-covered range of mountains, Lakeview (like Klamath Falls to the west) sits over an active geothermal area. Some local buildings tap this natural heat source, and Oregon's only continuously spouting geyser, "Old Perpetual," is located at the north edge of town. Lakeview's name refers to neighboring Goose Lake, which extends south into California.

Northeast of Lakeview, approximately 25 miles, the long basin of the Warner Valley combines shallow, alkaline lakes, marshes, playas, sand dunes, sagebrush flats and ranches. Like the Malheur country, these waters attract large numbers of waterfowl and other animals. A huge

Above: Big Alvord Creek drains snowmelt into the landlocked Alvord Basin beneath Steens Mountain in Harney County. DAVID JENSEN
Top left: A young ranch hand rests at day's end. GREGORY J. LAWLER
Left: The timeless routine of cattle ranching. BRYAN PETERSON

The view to South Mountain from the Hart Mountain Range seems to evaporate into the distance.
© GARY BRAASCH

fault-block escarpment, Poker Jim Ridge, towers above the eastern edge of the Warner Valley like a gargantuan basalt wall. A scenic gravel road climbs to the rim, where 275,000-acre Hart Mountain National Antelope Refuge spreads across the open, high plateau.

Besides containing some of North America's largest herds of pronghorn antelope, the refuge supports more than 300 species of wildlife. Ranging from the plateau's rangelands to the summit of 8,065-foot Hart Mountain, an intriguing array of changing environments host sage-brush plains, grasslands, streams, hot springs, aspen groves, juniper woods, small stands of ponderosa pine and green meadows. At the refuge headquarters, a display of the local flora and fauna, with brochures and maps, aid visitors in finding camping sites and seeing wildlife such as the elusive bighorn sheep.

To the Northwest of Hart Mountain, two other fault-block rims overlook lakes. In the distant past, these rims formed the shorelines of much larger ice-age bodies of water. Abert Rim, which rises for 30 miles along the eastern shore of salty Lake Abert, is the largest exposed fault in North America. Not far to the west, just beyond Wildcat Mountain, Summer Lake consists of seasonal playas and marshy areas below east-facing Winter Ridge. This fault scarp differs greatly from the arid rims to the east—it is topped by thick pine forest, bordering the broad timberlands that extend westward to the Cascade Mountains. The abrupt contrast between the arid Great Basin desert sand dunes at the east side of the lake and the green woodlands high above the western shore, dramatically delineates the point at which Pacific winds lose the last of their moisture.

This large, parched basin, known by early pioneers as the Great Sandy Desert, extends northward to the Millican Valley and the pine-clad Maury and Ochoco mountains. Incongruous as it may seem, situated in the middle of this open expanse a small retirement settlement huddles around a restaurant lodge, man-made lake and green, desert-surrounded golf course. Christmas Valley, though lacking the evergreen trees its name might suggest, does abound in a healthful, invigorating and sunny climate with low land costs and taxes and plenty of peace and quiet. A California land development firm started the community in 1961 and advertised lots to prospective retirees from that state. No doubt visualizing Oregon's famed green forests, several thousand people purchased, sight unseen, their own bits of paradise along streets named for trees that cannot grow there. Upon visiting their pieces of arid real estate, many disappointed buyers demanded refunds, and lawsuits proliferated.

Just 15 miles east of Christmas Valley, aptly named Fossil Lake preserves the dry remains of a large prehistoric reservoir, where pioneer paleontologists found early horses, elephants, camels, birds, fish and other animals in the late 1800s. Fossil Lake's 12,000 acres of huge, barren, wind-whipped sand dunes are constantly shifting to expose more relics from Oregon's distant past. Archaeologists also have uncovered from the lake bed the fossilized bones of a camel that appears to have been killed by prehistoric man. If this is verified, it would make Fossil Lake even more special, since few sites in the world bear evidence of humans coexisting with now-extinct Pleistocene animals.

At the northeastern edge of the Fossil Lake dunes there remains, for now, an interesting anomaly, Lost Forest. This 9,000-acre stand of ponderosa pine grows in an arid High Desert area that often receives as little as eight

Bighorn sheep on Hart Mountain thrive where few other animals even can travel. JERRY LONG

inches of rain in a year. Normally, these trees require from 18 to 30 inches of precipitation. Just how have they managed to survive here, isolated nearly 40 miles from the nearest pine forests to the west? Probably they are a remnant of a large Pleistocene forest that once covered the entire region. A study in the 1950s indicated that a hard chalk-like layer (probably an ancient lake bed) underlying the surface sand may trap and concentrate scant rainfall and act as a moisture reservoir. Additionally, conditions are drier now than in former years: "old timers" remember springs that ran year-round in Lost Forest 50 years ago. This forest eventually will vanish as the encroaching sand dunes from Fossil Lake slowly cover the area and the trend toward increased aridity continues.

Surprises—such as Lost Forest's welcome shade, Christmas Valley's green golf course, Malheur Lake's marshes

Malheur Wildlife Refuge

A Natural Heritage

Above: *Photographer and conservationist William L. Finley in the Malheur preserve in 1908.* FINLEY NEG. A2289, OREGON HISTORICAL SOCIETY
Right: *Blue heron.* DARRELL GULIN
Facing page: *Small Harney Valley lakes like this one in the Malheur National Wildlife Refuge attract 300 species of birds.* D.C. LOWE

In the early first glimmerings that portend a High Desert spring, when the ice begins to melt on Malheur and Harney lakes in February, the ages-old cycle recurs. The first pintail ducks come winging in on their annual migration north. And, as if a floodgate had opened, a virtual deluge of winged, feathered bodies soon arrives in their wake. Canada geese, snow geese, white-fronted geese, sandhill cranes, tundra swans and many other species descend in large flocks and the marshes come alive with the movements and sounds of nesting birds.

By early summer, the variety of birds at the Malheur National Wildlife Refuge is astounding. Broods of young explore the vegetation of the marshes. Observant birders and photographers focus their field glasses and cameras on such species as great blue herons, white-faced ibis, double-crested cormorants, white pelicans, many kinds of ducks, black-crowned night herons, avocets, willets, long-billed curlews, Wilson's phalaropes, common snipes, snowy egrets, western grebes, American bitterns, northern harriers (marsh hawks), marsh wrens and red-winged and yellow-headed blackbirds. Nesting birds of prey, such as golden eagles, red-tailed hawks and great horned owls, frequent surrounding trees and rimrocks.

Clanging Canada geese herald the southward migration in the golden autumn. The quacking, honking and whistling of mallard ducks, tundra swans, sandhill cranes and other species join the cacophony.

Anyone visiting this refuge during migrations will be amazed and uplifted by this spectacle of birdlife. Yet these birds represent only a small portion of the immense migrations along the West Coast of North America on the great Pacific Flyway, from the Arctic Circle to the Mexican border. Equally impressive, as well as sad, is the fact that this congregation of birds does not compare to the numbers the first white explorers saw when they entered the Harney Basin in the early 1800s. Due to various human pressures (both known and unknown), the original continental populations of migratory species is declining at an alarming rate.

At the turn of the century, hunters shot birds in unrestricted numbers, while plume hunters killed egrets, swans, herons and grebes statewide to provide decorative feathers for women's stylish hats. Egrets were totally exterminated at Malheur, while other species' popula-tions sank to dangerous lows. Early naturalists and the fledgling Oregon Audubon Society in Portland, decrying this unlimited slaughter, publicized the situation in newspapers and magazines. When pioneer wildlife photographers William L. Finley (who later became a prime mover and initial director of the new Oregon Fish and Game Commission) and Herman Bohlman sent their Oregon bird photos to President Theodore Roosevelt, he was immensely impressed. The pictures of vast flocks of nesting birds and the shocking evidence of decimations by plume hunters moved Roosevelt to include Oregon's first wildlife refuges into a new Federal Wildlife Refuge System. Three Arch Rocks on the Oregon Coast became a refuge in 1907 and Lower Klamath and Malheur refuges were protected in 1908.

Further additions of land enlarged the Malheur Refuge to 185,000 acres, one of the nation's largest bird sanctuaries. Three hundred species of birds have been observed on the refuge to date, along with 58 species of mammals.

Malheur National Wildlife Refuge, scenically situated at the base of Steens Mountain, 30 miles south of Burns, offers informational brochures, guide maps and a small museum with displays, at the refuge headquarters.

and teeming bird life, Hart Mountain's rich assortment of wildlife and.Steens Mountain's aspen groves, meadows and lakes—all contribute to destroy the persistent stereotype that Southeastern Oregon's desert is a lifeless wasteland to avoid. And apparently the word is out. The High Desert is suddenly popular, acquiring many new visitors and friends.

A newly formed group, the Oregon Natural Desert Association, based in Bend, seeks to further knowledge, appreciation and protection of the state's arid regions. Hikers wishing to avoid the crowded forest trails of the Cascade Mountains and enjoy backpacking in the solitude of the High Desert can obtain informational guide maps from the Desert Trails Association in Burns. A new, 130-mile route through Southeastern Oregon, now officially part of the Oregon State Recreational Trails System, eventually may be incorporated into a National Desert Hiking Trail that will traverse the West's arid sections. Presently, the Bureau of Land Management is assessing the suitability of several desert areas for wilderness designation, such as the Steens Mountain/Pueblo Mountains district, Hart Mountain, Abert Rim, Sheepshead Mountains and Trout Creek Mountains. Conservation groups even talk of someday proposing a Steens Mountain National Preserve that would include the Alvord Desert. A similar plan targets sections of the Owyhee River Canyon in both Oregon and Idaho.

Desert hiking, since most of these areas are at lower elevation than alpine wildernesses, easily accommodates the early spring and late autumn seasons. Despite scarce drinking water and occasionally harsh climates, the High Desert, far from centers of population, offers a refreshingly different outdoor alternative that can ease the strain on popular forested areas currently being "loved to death."

Even if one visits the High Desert only rarely, it is reassuring to know that it is there. In an increasingly hectic, high-tech, complicated world, Southeastern Oregon's solitude and spacious beauty well may become one of the state's most cherished resources.

Above: *The Lost Forest's ponderosas flourish in the middle of a desert.* ALAN D. ST. JOHN

Left: *The Owyhee River persistently carves its gorge deeper into the Southeastern Oregon landscape.* DAVID JENSEN

Facing page: *Blitzen Valley and Steens Mountain from Buena Vista Viewpoint, Malheur National Wildlife Refuge.* LARRY ULRICH

Sagebrush

Above: *The superbly adapted sagebrush.* BILL STORMONT
Facing page: *Sagebrush and juniper share the landscape below the Warner Mountains with an old ranch that was less hardy.*
GEORGE WUERTHNER

The distinctive, aromatic odor of sagebrush signifies Eastern Oregon's High Desert to most people. Seas of the gray-green bushes spread endlessly toward the dry horizons or crowd against the bases of basalt rimrock walls. Although sagebrush is associated with deserts, it actually cannot grow in the extremely arid, alkaline soils of true desert basins. But the High Desert is a semi-arid steppelands, and so sagebrush thrives in these grassy, high-plateau environments of various parts of the world. The steppe country of Asia, very similar in appearance to Southeastern Oregon, supports its own species of sagebrush that differ little from those native to North America.

This plant typical of the most remote, wildest sections of the earth derived its genus name, *Artemisia,* from the Greek goddess of wild nature, Artemis. Several species of sagebrush occur in Oregon, but by far the most common and widespread is the big sagebrush *(Artemisia tridentata),* which varies greatly in size, ranging from small bushes less than a foot tall in dry, rocky areas, to tree-like, eight-feet-high bushes in deeper, moister soils.

Superbly adapted to a dry climate, the small leaves of big sagebrush limit surface loss of precious moisture. A covering of fine hair reflects sunlight and further retards moisture loss. Its root system employs a twofold method of extracting maximum moisture from its environment. A shallow network of roots spreads out horizontally just beneath the soil's surface to collect rainwater quickly before it evaporates, while robust penetrating roots grow deeply into the earth to tap underground reservoirs. In some areas, big sagebrush comprises 80 percent of the local plant community, with as many as 7,000 individual bushes per acre.

Each year, in late summer and early fall, sagebrush produces small, yellowish blossoms. Allergy sufferers who moved to the High Desert to avoid the heavy pollens of Western Oregon's lush valleys sadly discover the pollen of these bushes. Nevertheless, sagebrush is a popular symbol of the open West and Nevada has designated its blossom the state flower.

The Paiute people used sagebrush in ingenious ways to adapt their rugged lifestyle to the harsh environment. Paiutes were a nomadic people who moved from one area to another to utilize various food sources, and their temporary shelters often incorporated sagebrush. During cold winter months, men wore leggings made of sagebrush bark and women often dressed in sagebrush skirts. Footwear consisted of well crafted, durable sandals made of the all-purpose sagebrush bark. In 1938, Dr. Luther Cressman and a team of University of Oregon anthropologists unearthed similar sandals in Fort Rock Cave in Northern Lake County. Radiocarbon dating showed these to be 9,000 years old, made by an unknown, aboriginal people.

Since the coming of white settlers in the 1800s, many changes have affected sagebrush country. Fire suppression and long-term heavy grazing in Eastern Oregon have reduced competing native grasses and allowed sagebrush to extend its range. Cattle ranchers and government programs, attempting to eradicate sagebrush in large areas, replant with exotic forage grasses. This practice has sparked controversy between conservation groups and the cattle industry in recent years, while disputes about proper grazing levels on Oregon's "natural" sagebrush rangelands still fuel hot debate.

PART IV

Northeastern Oregon

Gold Mines, Wheat, Pines & Granite Peaks

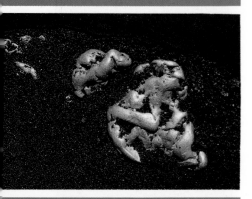

Above: Gold nuggets in black sand. NEAL AND MARY JANE MISHLER *Right: Oceans of wheat fill the Grande Ronde Valley near Summerville.* LARRY ULRICH *Facing page, top left: The Matterhorn juts above the Eagle Cap Wilderness, Wallowa Mountains.* LARRY ULRICH *Bottom: Cove's Ascension Episcopal Church dates from 1875.* DAVID JENSEN *Right: North Minam River and lush grassland.* D.C. LOWE

From Nez Perce Appaloosas to the Iron Horse Railroad

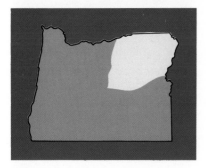

The earth was created without lines of demarcation and it is no man's business to divide it.

Chief Joseph

The wise chief of the Wallowa band of Nez Perce knew the region in which he lived. Although divided from the adjoining Northwestern states by a man-made state boundary, mountainous Northeastern Oregon differs from the rest of Oregon, having more in common with the northern Rocky Mountain region of Idaho and Montana.

Glaciated valleys, forested with the same mix of trees found in the Rockies, extend up to white granite crags, domes and cirques. Carpeting the rolling, open foothills are grasses, not the extensive sagebrush of the wide Central and Southeastern Oregon flats. In fact, large level areas of any kind are rare here. Most of Northeastern Oregon "stands on end." Except for the open Columbia River Plateau in the northern section, mountains rising between 9,000 and 10,000 feet dominate the landscape: the Wallowa Mountains, and the Blue Mountains complex with its many ranges. Like giant, white jagged teeth, these grand upthrusts soar from green forest mantles to above timberline. Interlaced between these ranges are small- to moderate-sized valleys nestled into the lower hills. The spectacular Grand Canyon of the Snake River, the deepest gorge in the nation, traces the eastern edges of this vast territory of wild peaks.

When the Lewis and Clark Expedition worked its way along the Snake River Canyon in 1805, following what later became part of the Oregon-Washington-Idaho boundaries, they met Native American Indians whose tribes had lived in this remote land for thousands of years. Divided into various bands, the largest tribes included the Nez Perce of the Wallowa area, the Cayuse of the Columbia Plateau and northern Blue Mountains, and the Shoshone and Paiutes of the southern Blue Mountains and northern Great Basin. Most of these bands were nomadic and tribal boundaries were fluid, as reflected in Chief Joseph's remarks about dividing the earth. To the communal Native American, the concept of owning land was totally alien.

Because the first white explorers and mountain men only passed through and made no lasting marks upon the land, the Indians usually welcomed them. Tribes trustingly fed these new light-skinned people, traded their furs to them and acted as guides, showing them ancient trails and hunting grounds. Unfortunately, these newcomers brought with them previously unknown diseases against which the Indians had no immunity. Thousands died. Whole villages disappeared.

The Eastern Oregon Indians already had acquired horses many years before their initial contact with whites, by trading with the Plains Indians from east of the Rocky Mountains. The Comanches of the southern plains had acquired the first horses in raids on Spanish settlements in Mexico in the 1700s. From this initial stock, horses soon spread throughout tribes of the interior West. In a related development, Eastern Oregon Indians also adopted another plains tribe innovation, the tipi. With the combination of the horse and this portable shelter, Eastern Oregon Indians traveled to distant modern-day Montana to hunt buffalo and trade with other tribes.

The first white men to explore the interior sections of Northeastern Oregon were adventurous fur trappers, many of them tough French-Canadian voyageurs. John Jacob Astor's Pacific Fur Company sent two groups to Oregon in 1811. One party went there first by ship, arriving in November, and constructed a fort and trading post on the coast near the mouth of the Columbia River.

This became the settlement of Astoria. The second group traveled overland, led by Wilson Price Hunt. They started from St. Joseph, Missouri on April 20, 1811, and reached the Snake River in December. The expedition included 32 white men, three Indians and the family of one French trapper: two small children and his pregnant Indian wife. By the time the party reached Oregon Territory, they were short of food and exhausted from the long, hazardous trip. At first they attempted to reach the Columbia River by passing north through the gorge of the Snake River Canyon, but they soon abandoned the precipitous route when it proved too difficult for their trail-worn horses. They struck off to the northwest, following closely what would be the Oregon Trail. In what probably was the Baker Valley, the woman went into labor and the trapper and his family temporarily stayed behind. The following day, the family, with newborn baby, caught up with the expedition in the Grande Ronde Valley. A friendly band of Shoshone Indians invited the Astor brigade to camp with them there and they feasted on horse and dog meat to celebrate on New Year's Day.

After a two-day rest, the trek resumed over the snowy Blue Mountains. Sadly, the baby died during this cold, arduous climb and was buried on the summit, above the

Above: *Pristine Sunshine Lake reflects 9,595' Eagle Cap amid alpine surroundings.* LARRY GEDDIS

Right: *Snow drapes an old wagon and barn near Cove.* JERRY LONG

Columbia River. The bedraggled group followed the Columbia to the coast, arriving at the Pacific Fur Company post on February 15, 1812.

A few months later, seven of Astor's trappers, led by Robert Stuart, more or less retraced this route from west to east. They left Astoria on June 29, 1812, bound for New York to report their progress to Astor. Passing through Northeastern Oregon in August, they reached St. Louis on April 30, 1813. Here, again, was proof that a passable—though lengthy and difficult—route across the continent existed.

Within the next few years, other groups of trappers explored the watercourses of Northeastern Oregon for beaver and other fur-bearing mammals, and traded with the Indian tribes. The Hudson's Bay Company trapper Donald McKenzie led a large brigade of men across the Blue Mountains in 1818 and continued into Idaho and Wyoming. Peter Skene Ogden entered the John Day drainage in the western Blue Mountains with another group of Hudson's Bay Trappers in 1825-1826 and again, on a later trip, followed closely what became the Oregon Trail over the Blue Mountains. Also in 1826, the first trained scientist to investigate Oregon, Scottish botanist David Douglas, entered the region. He traveled up the Columbia River in June, collecting specimens of many "new" plant species (the Douglas fir honors this pioneer naturalist) throughout the rolling, bunchgrass-covered hills of Northeastern Oregon's open Columbia Plateau and into the forested Blue Mountains. Although he twice attempted to reach the Grande Ronde Valley, described to him by trappers, deep snow on the summit blocked his path.

By the 1830s, the U.S. Army began exploring and mapping the Northwest and at least two expeditions crossed Northeastern Oregon during this period. Captain L.E. Bonneville, on leave of absence from the army, led his own exploratory group of 12 men through the Grande Ronde and Wallowa valleys in 1834. That ubiquitous adventurer Captain John C. Frémont also led an army survey detail through Oregon's remote Northeastern corner, in 1843, on his assignment to explore the Far West. He and his men spent time in the Grande Ronde Valley, camping near the present site of La Grande, and Frémont commented on the area's agricultural potential in his later report: "...a place—one of the few we have seen in our journey so far—where a farmer would delight himself to establish, if he were content to live in the seclusion which it imposes."

But years passed before settlers tilled the rich soils of this beautiful oval valley that the French voyageurs had named Grande Ronde. Although reports describing the fertile soils of the Willamette Valley and the general wonders of the West were beginning to circulate in the East, the region remained a largely unexplored, primitive wilderness inhabited only by Indians and a few hardy trappers. Before 1843, only a small trickle of immigrants had attempted to make the long, hard trip to Oregon. But in the early part of that year, more than 500 people, 120 wagons and 5,000 head of livestock left Elm Grove, Kansas and, led by Jesse Applegate, crossed the plains, deserts and mountain passes to reach the Willamette Valley in slightly fewer than six months. The Great Migration had begun. The trickle of hopeful immigrants, with their possessions, hopes and dreams crammed into canvas-covered wagons, soon swelled into a flood. Wagon trains grew larger. Although the Applegate party had enjoyed plentiful hunting and rich forage for their stock along the way, the trail soon became a wide swath of overhunted, overgrazed land.

The Oregon Trail entered the state near present-day Ontario, where the Snake River flowed more slowly and provided several crossing places. One of these, where the Snake takes a wide swing around a high, rocky point, became a traditional camping spot on the Oregon side and immigrants named it Farewell Bend. From this point, the trail progressed toward the northwest, through the Baker and Grande Ronde valleys, over a 4,193-foot pass in the forested Blue Mountains, then down to the open grasslands of the Columbia River plateau and westward to The Dalles. At first, these great caravans of people only passed through the region, intent on reaching the fabled productive soils and mild climate of the Willamette Valley in Western Oregon. The rugged mountains, isolated valleys and dry, plains-like country along the Columbia reminded them too much of the difficult lands they already had struggled through. Few were tempted to settle in wild Northeastern Oregon.

The Oregon Trail penetrated the heart of the traditional lands of all major Indian tribes of Northeastern Oregon. Although the first small parties of exploring white trappers had elicited friendly interest, this sudden influx of large wagon trains brought hordes of white immigrants through the region, hunting along the way and depleting the land of needed game. Alarmed at these developments and realizing that the new invaders soon would settle more and more of Oregon, some tribes began attacking wagon trains. In 1848 the Cayuse began a particularly

Camping on the Oregon Trail in the 1870s. NEG. 5237, OREGON HISTORICAL SOCIETY

heated campaign of massacres and pillaging against immigrant caravans between the Blue Mountains and The Dalles. Settlers quickly recruited an army of soldiers from the Willamette Valley and the few communities east of the Cascades, and quelled the war.

Prompt army action averted another potential Indian uprising in 1856. Planning to wage all-out war to drive whites from their lands, a combined force of more than 300 warriors from the tribes of Northeastern Oregon met in the Grande Ronde Valley. However, Colonel B.F. Shaw at Fort Walla Walla in Washington heard of these plans and led 190 troops directly to the valley to stop the potential war. A bloody, day-long battle ensued, in which Shaw's troops routed the Indians.

Indian troubles and the lure of gold in California stemmed the flow of migrants to Oregon during 1848 and 1849. However, by 1850, the number of new settlers increased again. In that year alone, 55,000 immigrants came to Oregon. By the early 1850s, a few people began to settle along the Columbia River. Catholics built an Indian mission in 1847 on the plain between the Columbia

Chief Joseph and his Valley of Winding Waters

Right: Hin-mah-too-yah-lah-ket, Young Joseph to whites, at about the age of 20.
COURTESY DUANE AND WENDY ALDERMAN

An often overheard remark from first time visitors to the beautiful Wallowa Valley is: "I can see why Chief Joseph fought so hard to keep this place for his people!"

Because of the Nez Perces' valiant battle to remain in their ancestral Wallowa Valley homelands, many people assume Joseph was an aggressive warrior chief. Nothing could be further from the truth.

Born in 1840 in the high mountain valley that the Indians called the "land of winding waters," he was named for the meandering watercourses through the wide-grassy flats. His Nez Perce name, Hin-mah-too-yah-lah-ket, meant "Thunder Rolling in the Mountains." Tu-eka-kas, chief of the Wallowa band of Nez Perce, was his father. But the first white settlers in the valley called the father "Old Chief Joseph," so they naturally referred to his son as "Young Joseph."

When Young Joseph was 31 his father died, leaving him with these final words of counsel: "A few years more and white men will be all around you. They have their eyes on this land. My son, never forget my dying words. This country holds your father's body. Never sell the bones of your mother and father." Joseph, now the chief, was later to say, "I pressed my father's hand and told him I would protect his grave with my life...I buried him in that beautiful valley of the winding waters. I love that land more than all the rest of the world."

For centuries Joseph's people had fished, hunted, gathered useful plants, and camped in the Wallowa area. They spent summers in the high, cool valley at the base of the snowy white peaks and retreated to warmer, lower canyons along the nearby Snake River during winter. A large blue lake nestled in a glacial trough at the foot of the towering mountains. In summer, Joseph's people constructed willow-pole fish traps across the lake's outlet to capture salmon swimming upstream. The streambank tripod of poles that supported each end of the trap was a "wallowa," hence the Nez Perce name for the lake. After the white man brought cattle and horses to North America, the Nez Perce acquired herds and became expert horsemen, developing their own unique breed, the Appaloosa, with its distinctive speckled markings. Horses allowed them to make long journeys east, beyond the Rocky Mountains, to hunt buffalo and trade with Plains tribes.

The Nez Perce were proud that none of their tribe had ever killed a white man. They had aided the Lewis and Clark Expedition in 1805 and had befriended all other whites traveling through their country. Yet for many years the Wallowa Valley's remote location sheltered these Indians from the negative aspects of white settlement, such as new diseases, liquor and usurpation of their lands. The Wallowa band of Nez Perce continued to enjoy their traditional lifestyle.

Settlers began pressuring other Nez Perce bands in Washington and Idaho for their lands and, in 1863, the government requested the entire Nez Perce tribe to give up its homelands and move to a reservation in Idaho. Although some Nez Perce leaders in more settled areas acquiesced and took their people to the reservation, Old Chief Joseph and the leaders of several nearby bands in this remote area refused. They called the peace treaty a "thief treaty" and refused to sign away their heritage.

However, by 1871, when Old Chief Joseph died, the new young chief faced the first white settlers moving into the valley. Again the government requested that the Indians relocate to the Idaho reservation, but Joseph refused and moved his people instead to a less-settled section of the valley to avoid conflicts with their new neighbors.

Unscrupulous white ranchers often claimed unbranded Indian cattle as their own, but Joseph overlooked these injustices to maintain peace. Even when two ranchers murdered a young Nez Perce, claiming he had stolen their horses, Joseph calmed his people.

Nevertheless, settlers feared the Nez Perce and asked for military protection. Army troops dispatched to the Wallowa Valley in May of 1877 ordered all non-treaty bands of Nez Perce to move to the Idaho reservation. With sad hearts, the Indians left their homeland, meeting other neighboring Nez Perce bands across the Snake River in Idaho. Unfortunately, before Joseph's people could continue to the reservation, hot-headed young men from one of the other bands left the encampment without the knowledge of their chiefs and went on a rampage, killing a number of settlers. Army troops rushed to the area and the peace-loving, diplomatic Joseph and his people were unwillingly drawn into war. A four-month-long series of running skirmishes covered more than 1,000 miles of rugged mountainous country and ended with the Nez Perces' surrender during a freezing October snowstorm on a bloody battlefield in Montana. It was there that Chief Joseph is said to have spoken his famous words, "My heart is sick and sad. From where the sun now stands, I will fight no more forever."

Joseph and his people never returned to their beloved mountain valley. The dispossessed Indians were restricted to reservations, first in Oklahoma and, later, in Washington and Idaho. Joseph did make one brief visit to the Wallowa Valley in 1900 to visit his father's grave. While there, he asked the local whites to give the Nez Perce a small amount of land where they could live and build a school. The whites refused.

During a visit to Washington, D.C. to tell officials of his people's grievances. the wise patriarch eloquently presented his point of view. "If the white man wants to live in peace with the Indian, he can live in peace. There need be no trouble. Treat all men alike. Give them all the same law. Give them all an even chance to live and grow. All men were made by the Great Spirit Chief. They are all brothers. The earth is the mother of all people and all people should have equal rights upon it..."

Chief Joseph died on September 21, 1904, on the Colville Reservation in Eastern Washington.

Many modern-day Oregonians attended schoolhouses like this one near Zumwalt. DAVID JENSEN

River and the Blue Mountains. By 1851, a way-station–trading post occupied this site, too, eventually to grow into the town of Pendleton. A few immigrants on the Oregon Trail, tempted by promising land along the route, abandoned their goal of the Willamette Valley. In 1861, several adventurous settlers apparently agreed with John Frémont's earlier positive assessment of the Grande Ronde's agricultural potential and built cabins there. Within a few short years, the valley's population grew and the small villages of La Grande, Union, Cove and Elgin sprang up.

Suddenly, in 1861, discovery of gold near the present site of Baker ignited a gold rush and would-be miners swarmed into the region, many coming north from the goldfields of California. Auburn, the first white settlement in the new gold fields of the southern Blue Mountains, mushroomed to a population of nearly 6,000 exuberant placer miners. As more gold strikes were made in

Mining equipment pulled by a 16-mule team pauses in Sumpter.
NEG. 26838, OREGON HISTORICAL SOCIETY

end of the war, military camps were established throughout Eastern Oregon and halted Indian by 1870.

Growth throughout Oregon during this period was phenomenal, and the remote Northeastern region experienced its share of rapid civilization. Thriving gold towns demanded supplies and so entrepreneurs built roads, started stage lines and plied steamboats up and down the Columbia River between Portland and Umatilla City (with portages of supplies around rapids and falls near The Dalles).

Local farmers and ranchers within the region found the hard-working, hungry miners a lucrative market for meats, grains and vegetables. With irrigation, the dry but rich soils of the Palouse Hills along the Columbia River and the mountain-rimmed Grande Ronde, Baker and John Day valleys began producing crops of wheat, corn and other grains, and various vegetables and fruits. Cattle, sheep and horse ranching, underway since the first settlers arrived, expanded greatly during the 1860s. Lumber, too, was in demand for homes and businesses in booming communities during this exciting and exuberant phase in Oregon's youth. Small sawmills, a long-time fixture in many communities, expanded to serve a huge timber industry that came into its own around 1870. Cutters extended their logging operations farther from towns, certain that the supply would never end, so limitless seemed the vast, old-growth forests at that time.

In 1877 and 1878, two final battles erupted between Indians and whites. The first occurred when the government ordered Chief Joseph's Nez Perce band to leave their ancestral home in the Wallowa Valley and relocate on a reservation in Idaho. When a few young, impetuous braves rebelled by killing some white settlers, all the Nez Perce from the area were drawn into a 1,000-mile-long, running war with the U.S. Army that finally ended with their surrender in Montana on October 5, 1877.

The second uprising, the Bannock war of 1878, came about when the government opened an important food-gathering area on the Bannock reservation in southern Idaho to white settlement. Enlisting the aid of the Paiutes of Southeastern Oregon, the large band of Indians moved north through the John Day country of the western Blue Mountains, killing whites. The war lost its momentum, however, when other tribes along the Columbia River refused to join the Bannocks and Paiutes. When a group of Umatilla Indians sided with the white army and killed one of the Paiute chiefs, the war fizzled to an end.

the area, other mining boom towns burst into existence. Canyon City, along the upper John Day River, started as a mining camp in 1861 and by 1864 was a full-fledged, lively town with stage service from The Dalles. John Day, Prairie City, Dayville, Mitchell, Greenhorn, Granite, Sumpter, Bourne and Baker City: all were born during this period. The discovery of gold on the south slope of the Wallowa Mountains in the late 1860s swelled Sparta with 3,000 residents. Many inhabitants of these towns were Oriental, as miners imported large numbers of Chinese laborers to do back-breaking hand work.

With most of the region overrun by brash, zealous miners, serious problems between whites and Native American Indians became inevitable. A number of massacres during this period took advantage of the absence of local army troops fighting in the Civil War. Chief Paulina's band of Paiutes caused considerable bloodshed throughout the southern Blue Mountains, until ranchers ambushed them in 1867. When the army returned at the

The 1880s brought another form of transportation that energized some towns and killed others. Construction of railroad lines east of the Cascade Mountains opened Northeastern Oregon to the "great iron horses" of the big steam engines. Two rail systems, one from Western Oregon and one from the east, finally connected at Huntington on the Snake River on November 24, 1884, linking Portland with the east coast of America by rail. Many communities along the railroads became shipping centers and prospered; others that were bypassed often lost population, some even disappeared.

The stimulus of railroads connected to the outside world boosted agriculture and the lumber industry enormously, just as the gold rush period waned and many mines began to play out. Wheat soon became the leading crop of the Columbia plateau; not only did rail exports greatly expand marketing potential, but also revolutionary farm machinery could cultivate the soil, seed, harvest and thresh, magnifying the productive potential of farms. These amazing machines, first pulled by horses or mules, soon were powered by another innovation, the gasoline engine.

The wild days of the Old West drew to a close in Northeastern Oregon. Trains from the East brought a new wave of immigrants who settled even remote areas like the high, isolated Wallowa Valley. The Nez Perce Indians had been relocated to reservations in Washington and Idaho, and the white communities of Joseph and Enterprise were growing. After a brief economic downturn in the 1890s, Northeastern Oregon entered the 20th century with renewed prosperity. World War I in 1914 spurred demand for lumber and, by 1930, all of Oregon's modern railroad lines were in place and an increasing number of automobiles were creating a demand for improved roads.

The 1940s and 1950s saw a network of highways begin to probe the state's back-country areas. Indian trials up forested ravines, where moccasined feet once stalked deer, now were traced by the paved pathways of an automated age. The Oregon Trail become Interstate 84. This once-remote, seemingly untamable region of soaring mountains and deep canyons, where the Nez Perce people had lived without imaginary lines of demarcation, no longer was a pristine wilderness.

Above: *A Sumpter Valley Railroad steam engine rusts beside the remains of a dredge depot.*
Left: *Mining ruins at Cornucopia in the Wallowa Mountains.*
DAVID JENSEN PHOTOS

91

Mining Ghost Towns

Right: The dirt streets of Granite once boasted a 50-room hotel, four saloons and a Chinatown district.
Facing page: The old Nibley Company mill still stands at Whitney. BILL STORMONT PHOTOS

It is impossible to drive through the mountainous sections of Northeastern Oregon without noticing the almost palpable aura of the gold rush that swept through the region like wildfire in the late 1800s. After the initial 1861 gold strike in Griffin Gulch, near the present site of Baker, thousands of men swarmed into the area from the Willamette Valley and California. Small wilderness mining camps of tents soon became "boom towns," filled with zealous miners enjoying saloons and bawdy houses that lined the streets. The railroad to Baker City in 1884 and spur lines that followed stimulated another boom period through the 1880s and 1890s. But shortly after the turn of the century, the gold was running out and the mining towns began to die.

These fascinating and picturesque old ghost towns resurrect an exciting era of Oregon's history. Many weathered townsites retain a few year-round residents, some only summer cabins, a handful have stores and cafes. The Blue Mountains to the west of Baker offer the largest concentration of historical mining sites in Northeastern Oregon. Highway 7, a pleasantly scenic route, leads toward Sumpter into the heart of the old mining fields, and some particularly interesting ghost towns.

Auburn. During its heyday, Northeastern Oregon's first boom town ranked as the largest city in Oregon, with a population of more than 5,000 brawling, energetic miners, all suffering gold fever. Shortly after the first strike in Griffin Gulch in 1861, Auburn sprang into existence, and quickly became the original Baker County seat. However, by 1868, when the diggings played out, business moved a few miles northeast to Baker City on the railroad line. Virtually no signs of the town remain today.

Sumpter. Miners discovered gold at this site in 1862, and Sumpter remained a mining camp until the Sumpter Valley Railroad arrived in 1896. Then the town quickly grew from a small village of 300 to a bustling city of 4,000, called "Golden Sumpter" at the height of its fame. The city was named, with slight misspelling, for Fort Sumter, South Carolina, by five former Confederate soldiers who made the initial gold strike there. By 1900, it boasted 16 saloons, seven hotels, six restaurants, seven general stores and many other businesses, including an opera house that hosted dress balls. In 1917, fire leveled most of the town in just three hours. Today, Sumpter is a small, quiet community that awakens each July with the Sumpter Valley Days celebration, featuring a fiddler's contest, axe-throwing competition, black powder shoot, arts and crafts displays and other activities.

Bourne. Few buildings remain of this hard-rock mining center along Cracker Creek, seven miles north of Sumpter. In 1937, the stream flooded and swept away most of the town, originally called Cracker City.

Granite. The dirt streets of this community, located high in the Blue Mountains 17 miles west of Sumpter, lend authenticity to Granite. Many original buildings still stand, hinting at better times, when residents prided themselves on a 50-room hotel, a few smaller hotels and boarding houses, a school, church, four saloons, jail and Chinatown district. An old stone marker at the foot of the hill below town proclaims, "Gold was discovered here July 4, 1862." A few year-round and summer residents reside in Granite today and patronize the small store.

Greenhorn. Located 14 miles south of Granite in a remote section of the Greenhorn Range, Oregon's highest and smallest incorporated town sits at 6,271-feet elevation. Property owners with summer cabins in Greenhorn reactivated the town charter in the 1970s, making it a legally incorporated city with a mayor and other officials. Thus, Greenhorn has been protected by its city council from commercialization and retains its authentic qualities. Founded in 1891, it never exceeded a population of around 700. Only a few buildings remain today.

Whitney. Located 11 miles southwest of Sumpter in a large meadow along Highway 7, Whitney transported primarily lumber from its mill, as well as some ore from nearby mines, on the Sumpter Valley Railroad. Always a small town, it dates from 1901. Old mill buildings and a few cabins, some occupied by full-time residents, remain.

The Wallowa Mountains provide a panoramic backdrop to the town of Joseph. STEVE TERRILL

93

Land of Golden Wheat & Gold-Bearing Mountains

Above: *A picker crates juicy apples from the LeFoere Orchards near Milton-Freewater.* STEVE ANTELL
Right: *The days of Northeastern Oregon's wheat harvest are long, busy and rewarding.* ROBERT McKENZIE; TOM STACK & ASSOCIATES

From a speeding car, the view from Interstate 84 seems a golden blur. Fields of ripe, yellow wheat mount the rolling Columbia Basin hills to the blue skyline. Heat waves of the midday summer sun keep the distance out of focus. Billowing clouds of wheat dust follow huge harvesting machines as they crawl back and forth across the croplands. Dust devils spin through the cut fields, vacuuming up large columns of straw and chaff high above the dry, baking countryside.

The broad, modern roadway of Interstate 84 cuts west and east along the Columbia River through the heart of the Oregon Wheat Belt. It also follows the old Oregon Trail. To immigrants, crossing as quickly as their slow wagons allowed, the dry, open Columbia plains of the 1800s appeared lifeless and hid potentially hostile Indians. Now, irrigation and proper dry-land farming methods have transformed a seemingly sterile environment into the state's breadbasket. The rich glacial deposits of loess silt soils in the Palouse Hills northeast of Pendleton produce bumper crops of fruits and vegetables. The Columbia Basin also grows famous Hermiston watermelons.

The summer heat of the low Columbia Basin's plateau country tempts visitors to flee eastward to the cooler, forested heights of the Blue Mountains. However, this wide, open wheat country beckons, too, with short trips on I-84's side roads into patchwork fields and quiet farming communities. Heppner, Hermiston, Umatilla, Irrigon, Milton-Freewater and Pilot Rock typify these local trade centers. These smaller settlements usually consist of at least a grocery store–gas station combination and—perhaps—a school, grange hall, church and some homes. Reflecting the local economy, a large grain elevator may dwarf the cluster of structures below it. The history of the Oregon Trail and of the first Columbia Basin settlers comes alive in small museums many of these towns contain. A small community cafe and its local folk may acquaint visitors with the flavor and personality of the land and its people.

For those inclined toward birdwatching, three small wildlife sanctuaries nestle within these farmlands, attracting a rich variety of bird-life: the Umatilla National Wildlife Refuge along the Columbia River near Umatilla, the Cold Springs National Wildlife Refuge east of Hermiston, and the McKay Creek National Wildlife Refuge near Pendleton.

Pendleton, the largest city in the upper Columbia agricultural area, shows that wheat farming shares this country with cattle ranching. The local chamber of commerce promotes such slogans as, "Not the New West, not the Old West, but the REAL WEST." But this is not merely tourism hyperbole; Pendleton has been the real West for a long time. A 100-year-old western clothing store downtown houses saddle-making craftsmen at work. Ranchers in town to do some shopping shade their sun-tanned faces with their broad-brimmed, weathered Western hats.

The cowboy persona dominates the town for an entire week every September when one of the nation's most famous rodeos, the Pendleton Roundup, takes place. It attracts hundreds of cowboys, including some of the nation's top rodeo riders. Native American Indians from the nearby Umatilla Indian Reservation and other visiting tribes participate in the Western celebration by performing traditional ceremonial dances. Two museums near the rodeo grounds are open year-round: the Roundup Hall of Fame, with historical buckaroo exhibits, and

Mitchell is the largest town in the John Day Fossil Beds (Painted Hills Unit) area. JANIS MIGLAVS

the Vert Museum of Native American culture. Pendleton Woolen Mills regularly schedules tours for those interested in the commercial processes of making sweaters, blankets and other products. Although Pendleton is a plains community, the nearby timbered Blue Mountains supply a local wood products industry, a lumber mill and a plywood plant.

Just southeast of Pendleton, I-84 ascends to the top of the northern Blue Mountains on Deadman Pass over Emigrant Hill, where an incredible view to the west across the Columbia Plateau unfolds. An immigrant on the Oregon Trail, describing this spot in his journal, wrote, "The sight from this mountain top is one to be remembered while life lasts. It affects me as did my first sight of the ocean…from this point north and south there are no bounds in sight." When pioneers crossed this pass, they tied logs behind their covered wagons to slow their descents down the steep slope above Pendleton.

The patchwork farmland of the Grande Ronde Valley unfolds beneath Mt. Emily and the Umatilla National Forest. LARRY ULRICH

integral part of the community. The coming of the railroad to La Grande in the late 1800s made the city the area's prime trade center. A large lumber mill at the eastern edge of town seems a natural part of La Grande, considering its situation amid vast stands of timber in the surrounding mountain ranges.

The college campus, perched on a slope in a west-side neighborhood of homes, provides a good viewpoint to see the lay of the country. An interpretive exhibit by the school marks where the Oregon Trail passed along the hillside. From the green lawns of the college, the rich farmlands of the broad valley extend to the snowy peaks of the Wallowa Mountains along the eastern horizon. The Grande Ronde River wanders north across the flat valley floor until it leaves the large basin near the milltown of Elgin. Nestled along the Wallowa foothills at the eastern edge of the valley are two small communities: Union, with its stately, old, brick, Victorian-style homes, and Cove, which, as its name implies, is tucked, alcove-like, into the surrounding hills. Nearby Hot Lake, features a large, old-fashioned sanitarium-hotel by a hot mineral springs.

High Valley lies along the scenic top of a long dividing ridge between these two towns. The few farm homes in this quiet, ridge-top hollow open onto forested mountainsides at the edge of a secluded wilderness in the High Wallowas.

The Wallowa Mountains differ from all the other high ranges of Oregon. The entire range is rather round in shape, with 9,675-foot Eagle Cap Peak rising from its center like the hub of a stupendous wheel. Radiating from this elevated alpine crest are the main watercourses of these lofty, white granite crags: the Wallowa River, Sheep Creek, Imnaha River, Pine Creek, Eagle Creek, Catherine Creek, Minam River, Lostine River and Hurricane Creek. Other prominent peaks of the Wallowas, all ranging between 9,000 and 10,000 feet in height, include the Matterhorn, Aneroid Mountain and Petes Peak. During the Pleistocene ice age, glaciers covered the entire range and carved steep-walled canyons, knife-edged ridges, hanging cirque valleys and pointed, horn-like peaks and rounded knobs. The Wallowas resemble not only the northern Rockies, but the Sierras as well, with their glacially smoothed, dome-like mountain tops and green meadows scattered with huge, polished, white granite erratic boulders. Indeed, the movie industry chose Eagle Creek in 1968 as a location to film the musical *Paint Your Wagon*, which takes place in the California gold fields of the 1800s.

The highway continues eastward through shady pine and fir forests until it suddenly emerges from a canyon into a wide basin surrounded by high mountains. This is the Grande Ronde Valley, where I-84 immediately enters the city of La Grande. With a population of nearly 12,000, this largest community of the intermountain area of Northeastern Oregon serves as the cultural center for the region. Eastern Oregon State College, the only four-year institution of higher education east of the Cascades, invigorates La Grande. An interesting mix of the modern and old permeates the downtown section, where up-to-date buildings stand side by side with brick and stone structures out of the 19th century. It is easy to imagine miners, trappers, ranchers and farmers coming to town via horses and wagons to do business along the dirt streets. The railroad station, yards and roundhouse, busy with trains coming and going, still function as an

Oregon's largest wilderness area sits astride the top of the Wallowa Mountains: 361,000-acre Eagle Cap Wilderness, with a network of 480 miles of excellently maintained trails. These wind through wildflower-bedecked alpine meadows, penetrate deep and shadowy forests, follow rushing streams, climb awesome gorges, and cross high passes above timberline that offer top-of-the-world views. Cradled among the peaks at the heart of the wilderness, Lake Basin contains a multitude of intensely blue, gem-like glacial lakes.

Because of the incredible beauty of the Wallowas, hundreds of people visit the Lake Basin each year. As a result, many prime camping locations are showing wear and tear, some of the lakes have become slightly polluted, and "traffic jams" between backpackers and commercial horse-packing caravans occasionally occur on narrow sections of trail.

The lovely Wallowa Valley lies along the north side of the mountains—the "Valley of Winding Waters," the Nez Perce Indians called their ancestral home. Chief Joseph and his people may be gone, but their spirits live on in many place names. Although the towns of Joseph, Enterprise, Lostine and Wallowa now replace Native American tipi villages and are linked by a modern highway, nature still takes center stage. Few locations in the Northwest exceed the Wallowa Valley for raw, unadulterated, primitive grandeur. Towering snow-capped crags abruptly rise like looming walls above the open meadows and irrigated green fields of the lowlands. However, for those driving up the valley, the scenic crown jewel is saved for last. Topping the crest of a small ridge, just beyond the edge of the town of Joseph, visitors suddenly see the entirety of Wallowa Lake. This five-mile-long body of water lies in a gigantic, glacially-excavated furrow that extends back into the mouth of a large gorge in the mountains. The ridge that provides this first, almost startling view is actually the terminal moraine deposited by a glacier and now serving as a natural dam.

A rustic lodge, rental cabins and other resort-style accommodations cluster near a large state park at the south end of the lake. Situated at the base of the mountains where the Wallowa River flows into the lake, several trails lead off into the wilderness area. Commercially-operated horsepacking stations serve the lodge and a llama-trekking business in Enterprise offers guided wilderness tours.

A tramway lift carries passengers in gondolas to the summit of 8,256-feet Mt. Howard. This vantage point

Wallowa Lake attracts wildlife from the Wallowa Mountains and recreationists from the entire region.
LARRY GEDDIS

gives a grand view into the Eagle Cap Wilderness and Wallowa Lake. The towns of Joseph and Enterprise, beyond the lake, punctuate valley farmlands. A decidedly old-fashioned, frontier appearance marks these communities. In Joseph, a privately owned log lodge-museum-gallery houses art and displays on Nez Perce culture and the Old West. Wallowa Valley tourism boosters tout their country as the "Switzerland of America" and "Oregon's alps." Interestingly enough, recent geological findings indicate that both the European Alps and the Wallowas may be "exotic land masses" that originated from a common location and, after slowly moving by continental drift over millions of years, "docked" in their present locations.

The view to the north and east from Mt. Howard takes in a broad expanse of ridges and benches, mixed open

Tiny, delicate blossoms on Barton Heights survey huge, rugged mountains and vast distances above the Snake River in Hells Canyon.
DAVID JENSEN

grasslands and forests. These drop away into the canyon country of the Snake River drainage, containing the tributaries of the lower Grande Ronde, Wenaha and Imnaha rivers. In turn, these watercourses empty into the magnificent chasm of the Grand Canyon of the Snake River, the deepest gorge in North America. This mile-deep rend in the earth's surface forms the Oregon-Idaho border and contains the Hells Canyon Wilderness, where 1,000 miles of trails lead through the rugged canyon. This section of the Snake is protected as part of the Federal Wild and Scenic Rivers System. Another remote preserve, the little-visited Wenaha-Tucannon Wilderness, is reached by a trail up the wild Wenaha river. Only two small communities exist within this immense district of canyonlands along the Snake. Both hide at the bottom of deep canyons: the tiny outposts of Troy, located at the confluence of the Wenaha and Grande Ronde rivers, and Imnaha, along the banks of its namesake, the Imnaha River.

On the south side of the Wallowa Mountains, Interstate 84, still tracing the Oregon Trail to the south of La Grande, passes through the expansive Baker Valley. Hemmed on the east side by the shining white peaks of the Wallowas and on the west by the imposing, jagged ridge of the Elkhorn Range of the Blue Mountains, the Baker Basin certainly qualifies as a genuine mountain valley. Here the Powder River drainage supplies irrigation to parts of the valley. However, a good portion of the area remains dry, devoted to extensive rangelands for beef production. A number of large, prospering ranches occupy the Baker Valley, and two small towns guard the north end of the basin. North Powder, located on I-84, marks the turn-off to one of the Pacific Northwest's highest-elevation ski areas, Anthony Lakes Ski Area—noted for its dry, powdery snow and located between 7,000 and 8,000 feet up into the Elkhorn Mountains. A few miles to the southwest is Haines, where the Eastern Oregon Museum displays relics from pioneer days.

At the south end of the valley, Baker, the area's largest city, does not have the Old West appearance typical of Northeastern Oregon. The architecture and general personality reflect the small Midwestern farming communities of Kansas or Missouri. Many early residents of Baker had roots in Mid-America, so this influence may have shaped the town from its beginning. All in all, the community exudes an ambience, a traditional stability reminiscent of an earlier era: business buildings constructed of quarried stone, a tall courthouse clock tower, Victorian-style brick homes and shady, tree-lined streets. Although Baker got its start during the gold rush of the 1860s, this was no short-lived boom town. Before the mines played out, the town established itself as a railroad trade center for livestock ranching, farming and timber. Baker's population of 10,000 has changed remarkably little since the turn of the century.

As times and economies change, conservative Baker realizes its need to modernize and is attempting to attract small, high-tech industries and capitalize upon its rich history to appeal to the tourist trade. Reflecting this trend, the entire downtown business district has been designated a National Historic Site and the Oregon Trail Regional Museum has been located there. The U.S. National Bank exhibits mining artifacts and a huge, 80.4-ounce gold nugget.

Remnants of Northeastern Oregon's gold rush radiate from Baker, fascinating mining ghost towns sprinkled about the surrounding mountains and canyons. To the northeast, along the southern side of the Wallowas, sleep the abandoned boom towns of Sparta and Cornucopia. Unlike the north side of this range, where recreationists flock to Wallowa Lake, the slope above the Baker Valley draws fewer visitors. East of Baker, Highway 86 leads through open, rolling foothills that resemble huge, green golf courses during spring, scattered with the bright yellow blossoms of arrowleaf balsamroot. Antelopes frequent these grasslands, along with many birds of prey, such as golden eagles. The secondary gravel road along the top of Sparta Ridge offers exquisite views across Eagle Creek Canyon to the lofty masses of Wallowa peaks to the north. To the west, across the Baker Valley, the immense, craggy backbone of the Elkhorns shapes the distant horizon.

Sparta Ridge accesses the high sections of the Eagle Creek drainage, where roads penetrate to trailheads at the edge of the Eagle Cap Wilderness. Farther east, the Sparta Ridge Road reconnects with Highway 86, leading to the small communities of Richland, Halfway and Homestead, and the Oxbow, Hells Canyon and Brownlee dams on the Snake River. A side trip at Halfway leads through the green farmlands of mellow little Pine Valley and into the Wallowas, ending at the mining ghost town of Cornucopia.

The real motherlode country of Northeastern Oregon's gold-rush period rises west of Baker in the Elkhorn and Greenhorn ranges of the Blue Mountains and in the upper John Day drainage. Almost any hike through this rugged land of high, open-topped, rocky ridges, thick pine forests, meadows and rushing streams reveals the remains of mining operations. Old mine shafts, dilapidated cabins and abandoned boom towns where thousands of people once lived dot this largely deserted back country.

Highway 7, following the Sumpter Valley, leads into this remote land that exudes an aura of fascinating history. The route passes Phillips Reservoir on the Powder River on its way to the small former boom town of Sumpter. The jagged peaks of the Elkhorn Range tower above extensive areas of molded gravel and rock disgorged years ago by the Sumpter Gold Dredge working along the river. The huge dredge still sags at the edge of town, a disintegrating, long-necked, mechanical dinosaur. These dredge areas now reclaimed by nature and a state wildlife area, attract birds and other animals to cattail-edged ponds among the rock piles.

After the railroad came to Baker, spur lines built into the mountains in the 1880s and 1890s transported ore from the mines and logs from the many logging camps. In 1891, the narrow-gauge Sumpter Valley Railroad began

transporting loads to Baker and, later, was extended to the John Day Valley. Closed in 1947, the now-restored train, nick-named the "Stump Dodger," takes visitors on a five-mile scenic ride through the wildlife area at the west end of Phillips Reservoir.

Beyond the Sumpter Valley, steep roads climb into the back country of the Elkhorns and Greenhorns. Hidden in this mountain fastness, the relict towns of Bourne, Granite and Greenhorn stand like bleached skeletons after weathering a century of summer sun and winter blizzards. However, privately-owned summer cabins are in use and a few hardy, year-round residents still live in these communities and the surrounding canyons. When the price of gold increases, miners reactivate claims throughout the region.

In remote sections of the Blue Mountains, the Elkhorn Crest Trail follows the dramatic, razor-edged summit of the Elkhorn Range. To the southwest, the 121,800-acre

Baker, the largest town in the region, looks more like a Midwestern farming community than a Western town.
STEVE TERRILL

99

Above: *The combined city hall-schoolhouse of Granite in the Blue Mountains evokes a simpler, slower time.*
Right: *A dilapidated gold-mining dredge sinks into the gravels it once excavated near Sumpter in the Blue Mountains.* DAVID JENSEN PHOTOS

North Fork John Day Wilderness encompasses the high Greenhorn Mountains. Both of these areas draw fewer visitors than the more-popular Wallowas and usually provide greater solitude. A particularly beautiful section, the Vinegar Hill-Indian Rock Scenic Area, features trails following high, grassy ridge-tops that offer spectacular views of the surrounding country. Early miners called a huge, greenish point of serpentine rock on Vinegar Hill the "Green Horn," thus naming the mountain as well.

West of the summit of the Greenhorn Mountains, the vast upper drainage of the John Day River feeds 284 miles of undammed water, one of the longest free-running stretches of river left in the U.S. Lying like a long, east-west trough in this western section of the Blue

Mountains, the John Day Valley rises abruptly along its southern side to the peaks of the Strawberry Range and their small wilderness area. Like the wilderness of the Greenhorns, this high district of lakes and trails is lightly traveled and promises a greater sense of isolation than many larger areas more intensely used by campers.

A few towns line Highway 26 in the bottom of the valley. Originally mining towns or way stations along the old stage road in the 1800s, the communities of Prairie City, John Day, Canyon City, Mt. Vernon, Dayville and Spray now serve as supply centers for ranchers and resident loggers. As with most towns in Northeastern Oregon, government employment with the Forest Service, Bureau of Land Management, Fish and Wildlife Department or other agencies provides livelihoods for many residents.

The Old West does not seem so old in this mountain-enclosed land of beef ranching. Every spring, cowboys on horses drive cattle through downtown John Day, moving local livestock from winter range to summer pasture. Each September, the Kam Wah Chung Days festival recalls the gold mining days of the late 1800s, when Chinese immigrants who labored hard in the local gold fields made up a large part of the community. The Kam Wah Chung Building in John Day, a stone Chinese trading post built in 1866, now serves as a museum of Chinese artifacts from that era.

The John Day Fossil Beds National Monument reveals a far more distant past. It is arranged in three separate units along brightly-colored, eroded formations. The monument's visitor center is located at the largest section, the Sheep Rock Unit, near Dayville. The other two divisions, the Painted Hills and Clarno units, stretch farther downstream into Central Oregon.

The National Park Service characterizes this unique area, first studied in the 1860s by pioneer paleontologist Thomas Condon, as "an archive of ancient life." Fossils as old as 30 to 40 million years tell of an age when the now semi-arid landscape was a lush subtropical forest, inhabited by such exotic animals as rhinoceroses, saber-toothed cats and three-toed horses. When a series of volcanic eruptions covered the region with ash, these plants and animals were buried and sealed into what now is one of the finest paleontological sites in the U.S. Over vast spans of time, the John Day River cut its way through these colorful ash layers, creating unusual badlands formations and revealing the fossilized remains of Oregon's long-vanished flora and fauna. The visitor center, located in the historic Cant Ranch House, provides

interpretive exhibits, brochures and maps for self-guided trails.

The John Day country, with dramatic geological formations like the narrow chasm of Picture Gorge and the towering, eroded pinnacle of Sheep Rock, embodies the rugged beauty of the high terrain east of the Cascade Mountains. Here, in the heart of Northeastern Oregon, brightly colored rock formations offset the drab, greenish-gray sagebrush; gnarled, stocky junipers compete with tall, stately pines; prickly cactus grows side by side with delicate wildflowers; and deep, rocky canyons challenge high mountain crags.

Above: *Sheep Rock dominates John Day Fossil Bed National Monument.* LARRY GEDDIS

Top left: *Strawberry Falls provides a delightful rest stop for hikers in the Strawberry Mountain Wilderness, Malheur National Forest.* GEORGE WUERTHNER

Left: *Troy marks the confluence of the Grande Ronde and Wenaha rivers.* DAVID JENSEN

Thomas Condon

Frontier Paleontologist

Above: *A 40-million-year-old fossil leaf at the John Day Fossil Beds.* DAVID JENSEN
Right: *Paleontologist and teacher Thomas Condon.* NEG. 3667, OREGON HISTORICAL SOCIETY

While chasing a band of warring Indians through the upper reaches of the Crooked River drainage in July of 1864, U.S. cavalrymen made an interesting discovery: fossilized mammal bones and seashells embedded in the soft, colorful hills above Beaver Creek.

Intrigued by the discovery of marine shells in this high, semi-arid region of sagebrush and juniper, Captain John M. Drake sent specimens to Fort Dalles on the Columbia River. He knew the missionary pastor at The Dalles Con-

gregational Church would find these fossils of extreme interest. The unusual man of God, Thomas Condon, often roamed the hills behind the frontier town, carrying both a Bible and a geology pick, seeking inspiration for his sermons and studying rock formations. Along with his deep commitment to spread the Christian gospel, Condon also had an intense fascination with geology and ancient fossils.

Condon's paleontological zeal was so contagious that Drake's entire unit of hardened soldiers combed the hills that day for more specimens. In the letter that accompanied the fossils, Drake told Condon, "I found our camp converted into a vast geological cabinet; everybody had been gathering 'rocks'..."

Upon examining the fossils, the pastor immediately sought permission to accompany the next army detail traveling into the then largely-unexplored interior of Eastern Oregon. He joined an army escort that was protecting a caravan bringing supplies to the Harney Basin in Southeastern Oregon.

On the return trip to The Dalles, the escort passed through the John Day Basin. Condon was captivated by the picturesque, brightly colored hillsides eroded into fascinating columns and rounded domes. He found several excellent fossil specimens. He could plainly see where the river had cut down through the topmost layer of basalt lava and then, below that, into the soft, ashy deposits with their bands of red, yellow, green and buff.

The pastor soon returned to the area and began unlocking the secrets contained within these dry, sun-baked hillsides. Throughout several subsequent trips, Condon discovered numerous fossilized remains of animals and plants no longer native to the region. Proof unfolded of a past age of lush, subtropical forests inhabited by giant cats, rhinoceroses, immense dog-like creatures and a primitive horse with claws. Painstakingly, over a period of several years, Condon cataloged species of flora and fauna contained within the various levels of strata. His findings indicated that the region had once been submerged under a shallow sea. Then, as the land eventually rose from beneath the waters, successive forested periods, each characterized by its own animals, developed over spans of millions of years, finally evolving into open grasslands.

When Pastor Condon sent some fossils to Dr. John S. Newberry of Columbia University in New York, he immediately received a request to send an entire series of specimens. However, return trips to the John Day country then risked the dangers of hostile Indians. In a letter to Newberry dated May 31, 1869, Condon wrote of his study area, "I am hungry for a sight of that hill again, when no fear of prowling Indians shall compel me to hold a rifle in one hand and my pick in the other."

By 1870, Indian unrest had died away and the pastor-scientist was free to continue his work in safety. Before long, news of Condon's discoveries circulated throughout the world's scientific community. The nation's leading scientists and their respective institutions, such as the Smithsonian Institution and Yale, requested specimens. Eventually, several scientists—O.C. Marsh, Edward D. Cope and Joseph LeConte—brought colleagues and students to visit the now world-famous John Day Fossil Beds. Condon's career as a scientist peaked with his discovery of a Tertiary horse with three toes, subsequently called *Miohippus*. Ultimately, nine species were unearthed and one, *Miohippus condoni*, was named to honor its finder.

Thomas Condon, who immigrated to America with his family at the age of 11, was a greatly gifted, natural teacher. As a young man he had devoted several years to teaching before entering theological seminary, so he was well suited to teach again. In 1876, the University of Oregon opened in Eugene and asked Condon to head its Natural Science Department, where he spent the remainder of his life as a highly regarded, inspiring and beloved professor. He also served as Oregon's first state geologist and discovered significant paleontological finds in the shifting dunes of Fossil Lake in the High Desert of Lake County. Thomas Condon's legacy survives in the educational exhibits and trails at the John Day Fossil Beds National Monument and in university students who reap the rewards of his pioneering contributions when they study a paleontology text book.

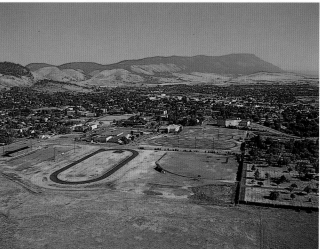

Above: *Picture Gorge wends its way through John Day Fossil Beds National Monument.* SCOTT PRICE
Left: *Eastern Oregon State College combines with La Grande to serve as the cultural center of the Northeastern Oregion region.* JERRY LONG

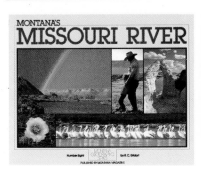
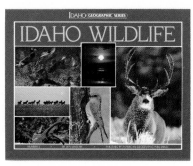

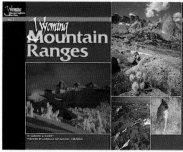

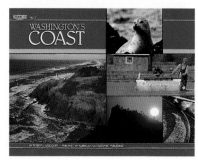